FREE-RANGE Kids

FREE-RANGE Kids

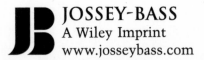

How to Raise Safe, Self-Reliant Children (Without Going Nuts with Worry)

Lenore Skenazy

JOSSEY-BASS
A Wiley Imprint
www.josseybass.com

Published by Jossey-Bass
A Wiley Imprint
989 Market Street, San Francisco, CA 94103-1741—www.josseybass.com

Jossey-Bass books and products are available through most bookstores. To contact Jossey-Bass directly call our Customer Care Department within the U.S. at 800-956-7739, outside the U.S. at 317-572-3986, or fax 317-572-4002.

Jossey-Bass also publishes its books in a variety of electronic formats. Some content that appears in print may not be available in electronic books.

Library of Congress Cataloging-in-Publication Data
Skenazy, Lenore.
  Free-range kids : how to raise safe, self-reliant children (without going nuts with worry) / by Lenore Skenazy.
    p. cm.
  Includes bibliographical references and index.
  ISBN 978-0-470-47194-4 (cloth)
  ISBN 978-0-470-57475-1 (paper)
  1. Child rearing. 2. Parent and child. I. Title.
  HQ769.S5519 2009
  649'.1—dc22

                                                                      2009004210

Printed in the United States of America
FIRST EDITION
PB Printing 10 9 8 7 6 5 4 3

Contents

Children) • Spoilage (of Lunch) • Sudden Infant Death
Syndrome (SIDS) • Sunscreen, Vitamin D, Skin Cancer, You
Name It • Teen Sex (Yes, Kids, We Know You're Reading This.
Now Come and Ask Us All About Contraception) • The
Woods, Playing In • Walking to School (or at Least the Bus
Stop) • Zoo Animals (in Cracker Form and Otherwise)

In memory of Genevieve MacDougall
All kids should have a Ms. Mac in their life

Acknowledgments

Since this book grew out of a column I wrote for the *New York Sun*, first thanks go to my editors at that late, great paper: Seth Lipsky, Amity Shlaes, and Katharine Herrup.

Amazing agent Mollie Glick saw the potential for a full-length book and shepherded it all the way through with bravado and encouragement. Let her be a role model to us all.

Beyond felicitously, I was snapped up by Jossey-Bass editor Alan Rinzler, who immediately felt like a long-lost cousin: same sense of humor, same outlook on life. We even look a little alike. He provided not only structure and wisdom but also laughs and chocolate. Hard to beat an editor like that.

The rest of the gang at Jossey-Bass/John Wiley & Sons provided the same exuberant support: Erin Beam, Paul Foster, Susan Geraghty, Carol Hartland, Debra Hunter, Michele Jones, Keira Kordowski, Mike Onorato, Erik Thrasher, Nana Twumasi, Karen Warner, Jennifer Wenzel, Carrie Wright, and everyone else there including—especially!—the sales staff.

For the speedy, meticulous research that made this book even possible, a huge thanks goes to Carey King. Time for her to write her own book now.

For inspiration, help, and kindness all around, more thanks go to Melanie Bradley, Trevor Butterworth, Dale Cendali, Gigi Cohen, Carl Honoré, Hannah King, Barbie Levin, Hedi Levine, Marla Sherman, and all the folks who wrote to Free-Range Kids with their stories, suggestions, and support.

This book would not exist without my family—and not just because I send the younger members out on public transportation. Thanks and love to my boys, Morry and Izzy, and to my truly better half, Joe, who is in the living room with them right now, teaching them how to do the taxes. It's never too soon.

Introduction

Welcome to—Yikes!

Y ou can't be too safe!"

That's the modern-day mantra when it comes to child rearing, right? A mantra that has brought us everything from baby knee pads (to protect kids from that daredevil activity called "crawling") to GPS backpacks (to track kids every second that they're not at Mandarin class) to the Cub Scout troop leader who demonstrated how to whittle with a pen knife, then handed each boy a potato peeler instead.

Just like Gramps used to whittle with . . . after he started wearing a chicken on his head. Trying to whittle a stick with a potato peeler is like trying to skin a moose with a pair of safety scissors. But "You can't be too safe!"

Or can you?

Welcome to the new and improved paperback edition of my book, *Free-Range Kids*. Well, it's not really that different from the hardcover edition, but it *is* softer, which makes it a lot less likely to accidentally bean someone. Phew! So let's call it the Safer Edition. It's also the Cheaper Edition, so you can give copies to all your friends who need to hear that there's a way to raise kids who are safe but also self-reliant—and that they can do this without going nuts with worry.

The whole idea behind Free-Range Kids is that we *all* want the very best for our kids. We want them to be happy, healthy, and eager as beavers to take on the world (if not quite as dependent on their front teeth while doing so). Lately, though, how we think we should go about child rearing has changed. For instance, I read a parenting magazine article that gave this tip: whenever you're taking your toddler to someone else's house, always carry a couple of shoelaces with you. Why? (One friend ventured, "So you can hang yourself?" No!) The answer is—really—so you can *tie shut the host's cabinets*. Yes, the folks at the magazine actually expect you to go around babyproofing the world.

That's not too much to ask, is it?

Free-Range Kids believes the opposite: the best way to keep your kids safe is to *worldproof your baby*. Or at least worldproof your growing children. That way they're safe even when you're not right there next to them, busy trying to turn the world into one giant womb. (And speaking of wombs, what's with those mobiles that play womb sounds to get babies to sleep? The kids are out now! Quit confusing them!)

Anyway, my point is that society has spent the last twenty years or so trying to convince us parents that our job is to make life into one big smoothie for our kids: no lumps, no bumps, just sweet perfection served up daily. The goal is to raise kids who go from colic to college without ever experiencing any frustration at all.

Smoothie mode begins at birth and explains the rash (so to speak) of baby wipe warmers. These gadgets are a baby shower basic, dispensing wipes as warm as the washcloths in Japanese restaurants. The question is, Do we really *want* to raise kids so addicted to ease that they are traumatized by a room-temperature wipe? Isn't that a little extreme in the "My baby should never suffer!" department? Don't we all want kids who can roll with the punches, or at least with some less-than-five-star diaper changes?

Of course we do! The funny thing is that even though none of us wants to see our kids suffer, seeing them rise to a challenge is one of parenting's greatest highs—and childhood's too. Even if it comes after, well, a little suffering.

For example, we all want our kids to learn how to ride a bike, right? It's a thrill when they do! Camcorders wait their whole lives for that moment (and then the battery dies). But to get to that peak point, we have to let go of the handlebars and watch our sweethearts take a few spills. Or at least we have to make our partner do this while we stay inside, eating cookies and reading books on good parenting. Still: someone has to let go of that bike. We do our kids no favor if we hold the handlebars forever. They need to develop self-confidence.

I'm pretty sure you can see the logic here. Helping kids? Good. Doing everything for kids? Bad. It's even a bad idea in terms of safety! Because, strangely enough, kids who aren't allowed a little freedom turn out to be *less safe*.

It's not just Free-Range me who says this. It's also Ernie Allen, head of the National Center for Missing and Exploited Children—the organization that put the missing kids' pictures on milk cartons (and made breakfast more depressing than a Nancy Grace telethon). As you'll see later in this book, I interviewed Allen about every parent's greatest fear—abduction—and he actually said that the safest kids are the confident kids. And the confident kids, he added, are the ones who have been allowed out into the world, where they develop street smarts and an air of "I can take care of myself." The safe kids are the ones who are independent.

Luckily, this is a book all *about* independence training. For kids and for the adults who love them. (And for the adults who love the adults who are smothering the kids they love, too.)

Now you'd think that this would be a rather noncontroversial idea. You don't see a lot of parenting books titled *Home Till They're 30!* or *The Saddest, Fattest Kid on the Block.* But it's not so easy to give our kids new freedoms, even when we think they're ready for them, because sometimes society disapproves. Sometimes the person who shares your shower disapproves. Sometimes the lady next to you on *The Today Show* disapproves, and you get the funny feeling that maybe the host does, too. At least, that's what happened to me when I was invited on that morning must-see to explain the philosophy of Free-Range Parenting (and defend my motherhood). It all came about thusly.

About two years ago now, I let my nine-year-old son, Izzy, ride the subway alone. I didn't do it because I was brave or reckless or because I had a spare kid at home (even though I do). I did it because I know my son the way you know your kids. He seemed ready, so after my husband and I talked about it, we gave him a map, a MetroCard, some money—and let him go. Then I wrote a column about it for the *New York Sun*. Big deal, right?

Well, that night, someone from *The Today Show* called me at home. Did I really let my son take the subway by himself? she asked.

Yes.

Just abandoned him in the middle of the city and told him to find his way home?

Well, abandoned is kind of a strong word, but . . . yes, I did leave him at Bloomingdale's.

In this day and age?

No, in Ladies' Handbags.

Would I be willing to come on the air and talk about it?

Sure, why not?

I had no idea what was about to hit me.

A day later, there across from me sat Ann Curry looking outrageously pretty—and slightly alarmed—because her next guest just might be criminally insane. By way of introduction, she turned to the camera and asked, "Is she an enlightened mom or a really bad one?"

The shot widened to reveal me and Izzy (stuffed with free *Today Show* muffins) and some other lady perched next to us on that famous couch, who, I soon learned, was there to TEACH US A LESSON.

I quickly told the story about Izzy's ride. How this was something he'd been asking my husband and me to let him do, and how

I think it makes sense to listen to your kids when they're ready for a new responsibility.

I know that riding the subway solo might sound like a bigger responsibility than, say, feeding Goldie the goldfish, but here in New York, families are on the subway all the time. It's extremely, even statistically, safe. Whatever subterranean terror you see Will Smith battling in the movies goes home when the filming stops (probably to New Jersey). Our city's murder rate is back to where it was in 1963, and, by the way, it's probably down where you live, too. Nationally, the violent crime rate has plummeted by about 50 percent since it peaked in 1992. In fact, as you'll hear in greater detail later in this book, crimewise our kids are actually *safer* than we were, at least those of us who grew up in the 1970s, 1980s, or early 1990s. (Yes, safer. And not just because all the kids are locked up inside, either. *All* crime is down, even against adults.)

So even though I did feel a little twinge letting Izzy go, it was the same twinge you feel when you leave your child in kindergarten that first day. You want it to be a great experience. And in this case, it was.

About one hour and one subway and one bus ride after we parted, Izzy was back at home, proud as a peacock (who takes public transportation). And, as Izzy tells Ann Curry on the show, it made him feel grown up.

Ann smiles and turns to the other lady, who is a Parenting Expert—a term I have grown to loathe because this breed seems to exist only to tell us parents what we are doing wrong and why this will warp our kids forever.

The expert is not smiling. She looks like I had just asked her to smell my socks. She is appalled by what I did and says I could have given my son the exact same experience of independence in a much "safer" way—if, for example, I had followed him or insisted he ride with a group of friends.

"Well, how is that the 'exact same experience' if it's different?" I demanded. "Besides, he *was* safe. That's why I let him go, you fear-mongering hypocrite, preaching independence while warning against it! And why do TV shows automatically put you guys on, anyway, lecturing us like two-year-olds? And where are *your* kids, if I may ask? Home hiding under the bed?"

Well, I didn't get all of that out, exactly. I did get out a very cogent, "Gee, um . . ." But anyway, it didn't even matter, because as soon as we left the set, the phone rang. It was MSNBC. Could I be there in an hour? Yep.

Then came Fox News: Could I come that afternoon? And MSNBC again: If I came today, would I promise to come on again over the weekend? Yep, yep, yep. And suddenly, weirdly, I found myself at that place you always hear about: the center of a media storm. It was kind of fun but kind of terrifying, too, because everyone was weighing in on my parenting skills.

Reporters queried from China, Israel, Australia, Malta. (Malta! An island! Who's stalking the kids there—Captain Hook?) TV stations threw together specials. Radio shows ate it up. So did parenting groups, newspapers, PTAs, blogs—everyone from *Nightline* to NPR to *The View*, where the ladies agreed, for perhaps the first time about anything, that I was a crazy, horrible, heartless, fill-in-any-disapproving-adjective-here mother. In fact, the media dubbed me "America's Worst Mom." (And now that my older son is thirteen, sometimes I'm dubbed that at home, too.)

But here's what's really wild. All that controversy prompted me to start the blog freerangekids.com. The blog led to this book. And that led the ladies of *The View* to invite me onto their show instead of just yakking about me in absentia. And guess what?

They'd read the book and loved it! Barbara Walters said it made her feel less guilty for having been a working mom. (Good!) Whoopi said it made her think—and laugh. Sherri Shepherd was out for the day, but even Elisabeth Hasselbeck seemed to approve. (Joy Behar I accidentally almost poked in the eye with my pen, so she was a little less enthusiastic. But still: she liked the book, too.)

Eventually I was even on *Dr. Phil.* We talked about how when we hover over our kids for their supposed safety, the message the kids get is that they're helpless without us. This may give parents a feeling of importance, but it makes their children feel like babies.

The audience, which initially held up a sea of hands when asked if they thought I'd done the unthinkable, seemed to take that in: the idea that if we have confidence in our kids and we want them to know it, we have to demonstrate it by taking at least a baby step back.

And that's what has been happening more and more as the Free-Range Kids movement takes hold: parents are taking baby steps, brave steps, and sometimes giant leaps toward preparing their kids for the world, instead of shielding them from it. (This book is filled with those steps, by the way: simple tips in varying degrees of bravery on how to get started going Free Range.)

Parents are excited to hear that there is an alternative to helicopter parenting. They're glad that there's an alternative to the fear and shame and neuroses-inducing *perfection* that had been demanded of them. They're happy to hear that they can relax a little bit and *everyone* wins, especially the kids. After we train our kids to look both ways, wash their hands, and never go off with strangers—the age-old lessons our parents taught us—we can actually give them the same kind of freedom we had. Go forth and organize a game of kickball, kid! Ride thy bike to the library! Frolic in the woods! And while you're at it, take out the garbage and rake the leaves, too.

These are not radical acts. Chores, games, and getting the heck out of the house were all a hallowed part of childhood until just recently, and together they help develop the very traits we want to see in our kids: responsibility, confidence, and good cheer. The ability to find something fun to do without depending on Steve Jobs.

In fact, play itself turns out to be the most important child development booster of all. If it were a class, there would be waiting lists to get in. Free play, that is. The kind our kids get rushed through after school because they have soccer, and rushed through after soccer because they have homework, and rushed through at recess the next day because they have to get back to class to study their number cubes. (That's what my kids' grammar school calls dice. For real. The fear is that if kids realize what they're actually playing with, they may quit second grade and run off to shoot craps for the rest of their lives. And we all know that it's just a small step from shooting craps to packing a potato peeler.)

Sorry. Back to *play*. Studies endorsed by everyone from the American Academy of Pediatrics to the United Nations have found that when kids are allowed free time to play freeze tag or explore the local woods or—best of all—make up their own games, they end up developing the very self-esteem we've been trying to Botox into them with praise for every doodle and trophies for twenty-second place.

The idea of raising Free-Range Kids reminds parents of what they already know in their heart of hearts to be true: that when a girl makes her own tree fort out of two old planks, she's more ecstatic than she'd ever be with a tree house built by Donald Trump. (Especially if he's in it.) That the boy who loses for three seasons at lacrosse and then wins in season four has learned more—and matured more—than any kid who was told, "We're all winners!" every single time. And that when our kids get lost and scared but then scrappily, happily find their way home, they come through that door three inches taller. And really hungry.

Kids are desperate to master the world, and we have always expected them to do just that. Until a generation or two ago (and to this day in less wealthy countries), children had to pull their own weight as soon as they could. They planted seeds, fetched water. During the Civil War, the girls cut their hair off to make money for Marmee. (Or at least Jo did in *Little Women*, and that's good enough for me.)

But today, in our understandable desire to ease their way and keep them safe, we've been doing everything *for* our kids. It's as if we've outsourced their childhood—to us! (Sorry, Bangalore.) Consider the fact that in some school districts, the PTAs have come up with a clever new way to raise money: they auction off the drop-off space directly in front of the school entrance, the sweet spot where kids have the shortest walk between car and class.

Now consider that if this spot were in front of a dentist's office or mall, it would be labeled "Handicapped Parking." In other words, for fear of kidnapping, cold, or just asking too much of our kids, loving parents are vying for the right to treat their children like invalids.

That's not really how we want to raise our kids, is it? It's time to believe in them again—and in our neighborhoods. And in our neighbors. And in our own ability to raise safe, happy kids without bubblewrapping them like hand-blown bud vases.

I know, I know—that's really hard. It's particularly hard to believe that our kids will be safe when so many of the messages we receive scream otherwise. "Is your toilet babyproof?" "Is your Barbie toxic?" "Is your child's rattle safe?" (probably not, if it's attached to a snake). We live in a world that uses fear to sell us products, toys, TV shows, even parenting magazines ("Playgrounds: Fun or Fatal?"). And I wish I could say I'm totally immune, but I'm not. I bought a baby monitor when my older son, Morry, was born—and we lived in a one-bedroom apartment. There was no way I could *not* hear him cry. But I believed that "good" parents bought all the gadgets. Then there was the time he was crying next to me in the car seat, and my mother-in-law said, "Give him a bottle."

"Are you CRAZY?" I asked. "The car could stop at any time. The bottle could choke him. He could be DEAD!"

I'd read that somewhere. Why I trusted some anonymous expert more than my own mother-in-law, who'd raised three kids—one so great that I married him—I don't know. Or, actually, I do.

Fear is like oxygen. We don't even notice it's there, but boy do we breathe it in. And so when we consider something as simple as letting our third grader walk home from school, friends and relatives raise their eyebrows. Some schools won't even let kids walk. One school in Florida has gone so far as to institute this procedure at dismissal time. The children are kept inside while the parents drive up, single file. On each dashboard is a card with the name of the child. An attendant in front of the school looks at the card and radios staff inside the building: "Jayden's mom is here!" At which point Jayden is *escorted out of school* and packed into mom's car. Next!

When that kind of evacuation procedure is considered just a good, normal safety precaution, you can understand why letting your kids do anything on their own is not something parents take lightly. What I usually hear is, "If there's even a one-in-a-million chance that my child could get hurt, it's not worth it. I'll . . .

"Drive my child the two blocks to school"

"Forbid my child to go on that sleepover"

"Keep my kid inside even though outside it is seventy degrees and sunny"

What we forget is that these "safety" choices are not without dangers of their own:

- The danger of childhood obesity, which has tripled since 1980. No one means to plumpen his or her progeny, but it's hard for kids to get in shape when they're not allowed to walk to a friend's house or even play on the lawn.
- The danger of diabetes. This disease is on the rise for the same reason as obesity: too much screen time, sitting time, Snickers time.
- The danger of vitamin D deficiency, leading to rickets. How did this Dickensian disease suddenly reappear? See above. Now add sunscreen. Kids aren't getting enough sun, and that's bad for their (now rickety) bones.
- The danger of depression. No one can say for sure why somewhere between 5 and 10 percent of all kids under age eighteen will go through this terrible illness, but it certainly seems that it would be depressing to keep hearing that the world is filled with creeps who want to kill you. Or that even though you feel you're ready to babysit, you can't even stay home alone for an hour because God forbid, who knows, what if? Or that you're not allowed to walk through a grove of trees or sit alone near the pond, even though time in nature tends to make most peo-

ple feel hopeful again. (I spoke to a guy from Tide who said that kids aren't even getting dirty anymore. That's bad news for him—and kids.)

- The danger of a college breakdown. Many of the kids arriving on campuses today are called "teacups" by administrators because they're so fragile. After literally a lifetime of overprotection, these young adults are overwhelmed by sudden independence. Sure, they're beautiful and beloved, and you can show them (and their SAT scores) off to company. But take them out of the china cabinet and they break.

Depression, obesity, loneliness, rickets—these are not what we mean to bequeath to our kids. They are simply the unintentional consequences of our fear. Some fear is completely justified, of course. But some is not. This book looks at where our fears come from, how to tell which ones make sense, and how to overcome the ones that don't.

What benefits do our kids reap when we can loosen our grip and let them be Free Range?

Let me tell you two stories. The first is about my friend's daughter, Carrie, a smiley, developmentally disabled redhead who is pals with Izzy, despite the fact that she's several years older. After Izzy took his famous subway ride, Carrie and her mom watched the story on TV, and a few days later Carrie, then sixteen, announced: "I want to get a slice of pizza by myself."

Her shocked mom said, "Uh, OK. But . . . why not get the pizza and bring it home to eat?"

"No," said Carrie. "Other people eat pizza at the pizza place, and I want to, too!"

God bless her, Carrie's mom conceded that point, and Carrie went off by herself a block or two away. When she came back just a little while later, full and happy, her mom was waiting outside, almost weeping. Not that she'd been so scared (well, that too). But that she was so proud.

And Carrie was even prouder.

The other story concerns a call I got a little while back from a man named Irving, in Queens, New York. He'd looked up my number in the phone book. Why?

He wanted to tell me about the first time *he* took the subway.

"I was ten at the time, and my mother said I could go, but I had to take my younger sister, who was eight. We got on the train and stood in the first car, so we could watch the tracks. It was winter, and the snow was falling. We were on our way to my grandmother's house in the Bronx. . . ."

Irving could still see it all, crystal clear. And when was this memorable trip of his?

1929.

Irving is ninety! He's been married sixty-three years. He has five children, and grandchildren, and great-grandchildren, and even two great-great grandchildren, which I wasn't sure was possible. He fought in World War II; he owned a business. But he called up to talk about this 1929 train ride because *it made him who he is*. He's the boy whose mother trusted him to do something kind of grown up when he was ten. And he's never looked back.

Free-Range Kids believes *all* children deserve parents who love them, teach them, trust them—and then let go of the handlebars.

The gift we give our kids is one that will serve them the rest of their lives. It is precious. It is thrilling. It is the foundation for a good life.

It's called childhood, and our kids deserve it.

Go Free Range.

FREE-RANGE
Kids

Part 1

The Fourteen Free-Range Commandments

Know When to Worry

Play Dates and Axe Murderers: How to Tell the Difference

It was one of those chaotic parenting moments. The ones when you have to make a decision—fast.

Isabelle, the twelve-year-old daughter of my friends Jeff and Sue, had just been in the middle school play. She was going with the cast to the local Friendly's for ice cream, along with several dozen kids and parents. Clearly this was the suburban equivalent of the *Vanity Fair* Oscar party, which is why Isabelle's little sister, ten-year-old Kaitlin, begged to go along too.

My friends said yes, even though they'd promised to look after Kaitlin's friend, another ten-year-old. Let's call her Baby M.

Sue had to peel off, so Jeff dropped all three girls off at Friendly's, gave them money for ice cream, and told them he'd come back to pick them up in half an hour.

So now, instead of going straight to Kaitlin's house as planned, Baby M was at an ice cream shop with her friend and another fifty or sixty riotously happy schoolchildren she knew. Being a responsible girl, she called her mom to tell her where she was.

"WHAAAAAAAAAAAAT?" screamed Baby M's mom. "You're WHERE? By YOURSELF?" She slammed down the phone and called Sue to yell, "How dare you do this to my child!"

Now look, I'm a mom too, and when plans change, I'd like to get a call. But there's a difference between being mildly annoyed and hair-standing-straight-up hysterical. The crazed mom barely had time to hang up the phone before she ran out to her car and sped over to Friendly's. She scooped up her kid—yes, leaving little Kaitlin by herself—but not before declaring to the world (or at least to a whole lot of ice cream eaters): "This is NOT how I'm raising my daughter!"

No indeed! She's raising her to be a hothouse, mama-tied, danger-hallucinating joy extinguisher—just like she is. (Which, by the way, is why I've changed everyone's name in this story. I don't want to make a crazed mom crazier.)

Days went by, and this mom refused to answer any of my friends' apologetic e-mails. Why would she? To her mind, Sue and Jeff had done the moral equivalent of dragging her daughter into a forest filled with wolves, snakes, and unshaven guys lurching around with a jug of moonshine in one hand and a pickax in the other.

Baby M's mom thinks her daughter is just very lucky that nothing bad happened to her that scary, scary night. She also thinks that, as a mom, she was doing the only rational, caring thing: making sure her ten-year-old was supervised every second, every place, every day by a preapproved adult.

How *dare* anyone subject her daughter to that unscheduled ice cream shop experience? Mama didn't approve of it beforehand, she was not consulted, she didn't check the menu for appropriate foods, she didn't know who the girl might talk to—and it's quite possible that while there, her daughter might have had to go to the bathroom. God knows what would have happened to her there! (Cue the unshaven lurchers.)

Anyway, my point—and maybe I'm starting to sound as wild-eyed as that mom—is this: a lot of parents today are really bad at assessing risk. They see no difference between letting their children walk to school and letting them walk through a firing range. When they picture their kids riding their bikes to a birthday party, they see them dodging Mack trucks with brake problems. To let their children play unsupervised in a park at age eight or ten or even thirteen seems about as responsible as throwing them in the shark tank at Sea World with their pockets full of meatballs.

Any risk is seen as too much risk. A crazy, not-to-be-taken, see-you-on-the-local-news risk. And the only thing these parents don't seem to realize is that the greatest risk of all just might be trying to raise a child who never encounters *any* risks.

Not that I'm a fan of taking crazy risks. I hate them! They make no sense. Riding a bike without a helmet strikes me as about as sensible as riding a roller coaster rated MP for "Missing Planks." My love for seatbelts borders on the obsessive. And car seats? One of those saved my life when I was two and our car somersaulted off the highway. That was before car seats were even required, so I come from solid, safety-loving stock. Safety is *good*. But if we try to prevent every possible danger or difficulty in our child's everyday life, that child never gets a chance to grow up.

Or eat ice cream without a chaperone.

Now, if "The Incident at Friendly's" were unusual, this book would end right here. It would be about one overworried mom, and who cares about that?

But unfortunately, Mama M is not alone in her fears. Millions of moms and almost (but not quite) as many dads now see the world as so fraught with danger that they can't possibly let their children explore it.

Sometimes they regret having to rein their kids in, but rein them in they do. A woman who wrote me from quiet, suburban Atlanta won't let her daughter go to the mailbox by herself. That's right. The *mailbox*. In her mind, there's just "too much that could happen" between the door and the curb.

Another dad informed his daughter that he was going to follow her school field trip to make sure nothing happened to her. Why? Could he stop the bus from plunging off the road?

Then there was the New Jersey radio talk show host who interviewed me after the now infamous incident of my letting Izzy ride the subway by himself. How could I do such a crazy thing, the host demanded. *He* believes in safety. *He* loves his son. That's why *he* won't let the boy, age eight, play basketball in his own driveway. *Too many creeps out there!*

Yes, there are many creeps in this world of ours. Some of them even have bombastic radio shows and speak in italics. But some of them are creeps of the classic kind: pedophiles and murderers and guys who feel compelled to show kids what's under their raincoat. Creeps are a sad fact of life. The fact that many parents seem unable to process, however, is that

THERE AREN'T ANY MORE CREEPS NOW THAN WHEN WE WERE KIDS.

Hard to believe, but that's what the statistics show. Over at the Crimes Against Children Research Center, they track these things (as you might guess from their name). David Finkelhor, the founder of the center and a professor at the University of New Hampshire, says that violent crime in America has been falling since it peaked in the early nineties. That includes sex crimes against kids. He adds that although perhaps the streets were somewhat safer in the fifties, children today are statistically as safe from violent crime as we parents were, growing up in the seventies, eighties, and nineties.

So when parents say, "I'd love to let my kids have the same kind of childhood I had, but times have changed," they're not making a rational argument.

Times have *not* changed. Especially not where childhood abductions are concerned. Those crimes are so very rare that the rates do not go up or down by much in any given year. Throw in the fact that now almost everyone is carrying a cell phone and can immediately call the police if they see a kid climbing into a van filled with balloons, a clown, and automatic weapons, and times are, if anything, safer.

The problem is that we parents *feel* that childhood is more dangerous for our kids than it was for us, and over the course of this book, we'll look at where those fears come from and which ones are utterly baseless and why they're so hard to shake. But if you (like, sometimes, me) only read a chapter or two and then "forget" to read the rest of a book, or "accidentally" leave it on the bus, let me just state clearly before it's too late that we have it all wrong. Our kids are more competent than we believe, and they're a whole lot safer, too. We are extremely worried today about exceedingly unlikely disasters—or, as the experts put it, "negative outcomes." (Like death would be a "negative outcome" of gum surgery.)

Dr. F. Sessions Cole, chief medical officer at the St. Louis Children's Hospital, one of the Midwest's biggest medical centers, put it this way: "The problem is that the public assumes that any risk to any individual is 100 percent risk to them."

What he means is that if people hear about one child who died from falling out of a crib, they immediately assume that their child is at risk for that same thing. When one child gets a rare infection, they think it's likely that theirs could too. When they hear about one child abducted from a parking lot, they assume their child could well be next, even though, in reality, those chances are so slim that actual, factual statisticians have a word for them: *de minimis*. Risks so small that they are virtually equivalent to none. I'm not saying that the abducted children are equivalent to none. No! I'm saying that the risk is so small, it's almost impossible to guard against. Just like it's almost impossible to guard against the possibility of being hit by an asteroid.

And yet rattled parents, besieged by media and each other, feel they must take all possible precautions to avoid all these extremely rare possibilities. "But if you live your life that way," said Dr. Cole, "as best I can tell, you can never even go to the bathroom, because there could be something that sucks you into the toilet."

But Dr. Cole isn't being flip. He's the classic white-haired, sixty-something doctor—he should have his own TV show, he's so perfect for the part of himself—and over the past twenty years he's seen more and more parents coming in distraught about more and more outlandish possibilities. Even after he has reassured these parents that their child is fine, they demand MRIs and other tests to "prove" it. Or, just to be safe, they decide to restrict their children's diets, even after he tells them he seriously doubts this will have any effect on their health.

This eagerness to restrict things is not limited to food. Think of how, thanks to fear, we restrict so many other aspects of our children's lives. They're not allowed to walk alone (cars!), explore (perverts!), or play in the park (those perverts again) or in the woods (ticks!) or in trees (gravity!) or in water (drowning!) or in dirt (dirt). It's not your imagination: childhood really has changed. Forty years ago, the majority of U.S. children walked or biked to school. Today, about 10 percent do. Meantime, 70 percent of today's moms say they played outside as kids. But only 31 percent of their kids do. The children have been sucked off America's lawns like yard trimmings.

Where did all this fear come from? Take your pick: The fact that we're all working so hard that we don't know our neighbors. The fact that the marketplace is brimming with products to keep our kids "safe" from things we never used to worry about—like shopping cart liners to protect kids from germs.

Then there's the way our brains cling to scary thoughts (girls murdered on a country road) but not mundane ones (all the girls who walk home from school without getting murdered). That's just basic psychology. Meanwhile, "helpful" articles list the dangers of every possible activity from running barefoot (fungus!) to flying kites. "Choose a sunny day when there's no chance of lightning," one kite article actually suggested. So I guess we shouldn't choose a day when trees are flying by the window and there's a funnel-shaped cloud coming toward the driveway? Thank you so much, oh wise magazine!

Fear, fear, fear. We're always expected to be thinking about fear. Schools hold pre–field trip assemblies explaining exactly how close the children will be to a hospital. At least, our school did. Come home and the TV tells us about "the killer under your sink!" (Turns out you shouldn't drink Drano.) And "the monster who could be your neighbor!" (but probably isn't). And "the hidden danger in your drink!" (A lemon. It has bacteria on it. Big deal. So does everything else.) Everyone is exhorting us to watch out, take care, and plan for the very worst-case scenario. Which puts a damper on things, to say the least.

A doctor wrote to the Free-Range Kids Web site:

> We live in beautiful Ardsley, New York. I pay 20K in taxes a year to provide a safe environment and good education for my children. You would have thought I committed a crime when I let my 8-year-old daughter ride her bike by herself approximately two city blocks to a friend's house. My wife let it be known how vehemently she disagreed with me. In addition, all the parents in the neighborhood also thought I was crazy. Indeed, of course I would have grieved had "something" happened. But should I let that immobilize my children? I lost my mother to a drunk driver at the age of 46, and my sister to cancer at age 24. In addition, I am an emergency medicine physician who sees tragedy every day. Therefore, I know, more than most, the pain of tragedy and longshots. I could let this paralyze me, but I don't. I choose, to the best of my ability, to allow my children the same freedoms that I had as a child growing up, when I was taking the train by the 7th grade, and riding my bike by myself by the age of 9. I choose to give my children freedom.

What a cool guy, embracing life with his eyes wide open. Good luck to him, and good luck to you, dear reader, as you seem to be on the same journey. And then good luck convincing your friends and spouse to join you.

You're going to need it.

REAL WORLD

What's Wrong with Our Society?
What's Wrong with Me?

A Free-Ranger writes:

> I'm a mom of a 13-year old boy and an 11-year old girl and I'm ashamed of how paranoid I am. The news keeps you in constant fear of your child being abducted and raped and eaten, etc. I was a kid who took two buses to get to my Catholic School as early as age 7. And I did it all by myself. My friends and I wandered all over the city, and as long as we were home by dark, we could do whatever we wanted. Without cell phones! Now, here I am, with a teenager, and I get an upset tummy when I watch him walk with his friends to junior high each day. What's wrong with our society? What's wrong with me? Here I am, a fearless adult who went everywhere I wanted, and I'm too paranoid to let my teenager walk to the store. I'm ashamed that I've allowed society to shape me into a worrier. Yes, there are predators. But they aren't everywhere and I need to get over myself. Fast. Before I raise a scaredy-cat son and paranoid daughter. We're gonna have a whole generation of skittish people if we don't give our kids some space, starting with mine. I'm gonna go kick them out of the house on this sunny afternoon and let them wander. (But they better answer their cell phones.)

Going Free Range

All kids are different, as are all parents (for better or worse), but if you're reading this book, chances are you are probably wondering how to start weaning yourself off of excess worry and giving your kids some old-fashioned freedom. There are no hard-and-fast timetables and, alas, no guarantees of which of these will work for you (or me!), but consider the following suggestions:

Free-Range Baby Step: Cross the street with your school-age child, without holding hands. Make 'em look around at the traffic.

Free-Range Brave Step: Let your little bikers, starting at age six or so, ride around the block a couple times, beyond where you can see them. (Yes, in their helmets.)

One Giant Leap for Free-Range Kind: Drop off your third- or fourth-grade child and a friend at an ice cream store with money for sundaes. Pick them up in half an hour. So there.

Turn Off the News

Go Easy on the "Law and Order," Too

Is there one single reason we are so much more scared than our parents? One person, place, or thing that left us so shaken that we spend literally four times as much time supervising our kids than our own moms and dads did in 1975? Yes, and I'll give you a hint:

It has white hair, seems to be on CNN about twenty hours a day, and has piercing blue eyes so brimming with empathy that you want to hold him tight no matter what your sexual orientation. Or his.

Of course, it's not just Anderson Cooper that's driving us crazy with fear about crime. But he's part of the problem, just like cable news is, and local news is, and Larry "Let's Talk About Jaycee Dugard One More Time" King is. And Nancy G. And *Law and Order*, and *Law and Order*, and *Law and Order*, and the other *Law and Order*. The one with the special victims. Or, as TV historian Robert Thompson says, "The *Law and Order* for people who like to see crimes that are grossly sexually fetishized and practiced on children or vulnerable adults."

What's not to like?

The problem with all these shows, from the news to the dramas ripped from the news, is that they present us with a world so focused on the least common, most horrific crimes that we get a totally skewed picture of what it's like out there. How skewed? Let's take a look at the TV listings.

Well, hmm. This week you could watch a double murder on *The Mentalist*. That's nice. Then it says there's a "dismembered, headless body" discovered on *Bones*. I guess *Bones* did some test marketing and realized that a merely dismembered body might lose some viewers. ("Forget it! If the head's still attached, I'm not watching.") Then there's *CSI: NY*. The episode I just watched showed, oh, a guy's stomach sliced open because he swallowed a key. And a body dredged up from a swamp. Then there was a woman almost drowned by a madman in a bathtub, but she survived—only to stumble around and accidentally impale her breast on a towel hook. (I hate it when that happens.) On the local news right after that, there was a guy on fire, and a guy who plunged to death, naked. And *Law and Order* featured a fourteen-year-old girl raped by a Serbian war criminal. Well, we didn't see the actual rape. But we saw her going, "Mph! Mphmmph!" through the duct tape over her mouth as the leering guy reached for her thigh. (She was, of course, bound with a phone cord—like anyone still has a cord phone—and blindfolded.)

I'll get to real news shows in a minute, because we all know how they can make you feel totally depressed about the world. But less attention has been paid to the fact that even these so-called entertainment shows (Rape! Bondage! Towel-hook impaling! *That's* entertainment) end up changing our whole outlook.

The problem is that once we see horrific images, only half of our brain takes the time to say, "Wow. That makeup person did an incredible job with those puncture wounds. And hats off to the wonderful writing staff!" (If, indeed, any part of the brain ever thanks writers.) The other half of our brain just takes in those gruesome images wholesale and files them under "Sick World, comma, What we live in."

In his book *The Science of Fear*, Daniel Gardner explains that once an image gets into that "reptilian" part of the brain, not only can you not shake it, you can't extricate it from all the other images and feelings jostling around in there, either. After all, it's only been the last hundred years or so that the brain has started seeing realistic-looking images (TV, movies) that weren't directly applicable to its fate (lions, spears). So it hasn't figured out yet how to separate the real from the manufactured. Especially whatever's manufactured by Jerry Bruckheimer.

Thus the fight-or-flight, feel-it-in-your-guts reptilian brain treats *The Dark Knight* and a commercial for *Dexter* and the nightly news as one and the same. So when we are faced with a situation we think might be risky and we are trying to figure out what to do, it starts rummaging through all the horrible stuff it has seen and comes to the conclusion, "Jeez Louise! Look what can happen! Run for your life!"

Now, if you're wondering why our reptilian brains would be making us more scared today than our parents' reptilian brains made them just a generation ago, one reason is that when our parents were raising good ol' us, they didn't see this kind of TV. They saw *Bonanza*. Or maybe *Medical Center*. They weren't seeing dead bodies with realistic towel-hook holes in them. They weren't seeing all those autopsies on *CSI* or horrific dismemberments or decaying bodies dredged from the river. In fact, says TV historian Thompson, "I don't think there's a single episode of *Law and Order* that could have even been *shown* before 1981." That's because, until then, graphic images like the girl with the duct tape, rapist, and phone cord were taboo. In fact, they were the stuff of porn.

What happened?

In 1971, the rules changed. From 1929 up to that point, says Thompson, broadcasters held themselves to a code of conduct so strict that they couldn't even use the word "pregnant." They couldn't use bad language. They couldn't show a toilet bowl on TV. (That's why the Ty-D-Bol man was always in the tank.) Through the Great Depression, a world war, two nuclear bombs, and the civil rights movement, the material you could hear on the radio and see on TV stayed pretty much the same. Tame. Then, in '71, along came *All in the Family*.

That groundbreaking show became a huge turning point in our media and our culture. Every week, *All in the Family* broke another taboo. It talked about impotence, molestation, constipation. It flushed a toilet! And the ratings went through the roof. It became the number-one-rated show for five years straight—a feat never surpassed (though the *Cosby Show* did, later, tie it).

Naturally broadcasters said, "Number one for five years? Let's make five thousand of these!" So they started throwing in all the sex and grit and bodily functions they could. As did TV news. And let's not forget that, this being the seventies, plenty of social up-heaving was going on outside the boob tube, too.

In 1981, things lurched dramatically again, as cable TV came into its own and started segmenting the hitherto mass audience. You wanted to watch women writhing in leather bustiers? You had your MTV. Or your Playboy Channel. Or your HBO. Whatever. You had a lot of channels. You wanted weepy stories of women with unusual diseases? You had Lifetime. And if you wanted news all day long? You turned on CNN.

Let's stop here and think about what that meant: an entire twenty-four hours to fill with news. Every day. How on earth could you keep people watching the same channel for hours on end?

There is one proven and tested way. Pick a sensational tabloid story and treat it seriously, earnestly, gravely, as if all you really want is the best for your viewers. Repeatedly broadcast the same heart-wrenching footage, looping back again and again, right after this message, to create a sense of the most compelling, continuing, crying-shame story ever to dominate a news cycle. A story so grip-ping, viewers would feel almost guilty turning it off. A story you could drag out (like this paragraph) for hours and hours, days and days, even if you had only tiny crumbs of info to add. And to date, the best story anyone has ever found turns out to be . . . a missing child.

"Missing kids are everybody's fear," said a cable exec I can't quote by name because she's still in the biz (even though she's not happy about it). "Especially when there's a story with somebody who looks normal," she said. "People really respond to that. They think, 'That could be me.'" "Me" being a middle- to upper-middle-class white person, usually.

The granddaddy of this programming was the 1983 two-part miniseries, *Adam*, based on the story of Adam Walsh, a six-year-old boy who was abducted from a Florida Sears and beheaded in 1981. It makes me sick just to type that.

The series about him—a ratings blockbuster—introduced America to Adam's dad, John Walsh, who appeared with his wife at the end of the show with photos of other missing children. Walsh became a crusader for children's safety and went on to host *America's Most Wanted*. He also helped found the National Center for Missing and Exploited Children. You probably came of age eating breakfast with those kids.

"The whole milk carton phenomenon begins at this time," says Thompson, referring to the phenom of dairies printing the photos of missing children on their cartons—without even clarifying whether the child was kidnapped by a stranger (extremely rare), taken by a divorced parent in a custody dispute (more likely), or had simply run away (also quite likely). Mornings became pretty somber as we ate our Rice Krispies with the milk carton kids staring us in the face. In fact, it began to feel as if millions of kids were being taken, willy-nilly, across the country. And all together, this set the template for our modern-day fear of abduction.

That fear, as I'll say again and again in this book, bears no relation to reality. The statistics cited by the National Center for Missing and Exploited Children itself show that the number of children abducted and killed by strangers holds pretty steady over the years— about 1 in 1.5 million. Put another way, the chances of any one American child being kidnapped and killed by a stranger are almost infinitesimally small: .00007 percent. Put yet another, even better way, by British author Warwick Cairns, who wrote the book *How to Live Dangerously*: if you actually *wanted* your child to be kidnapped and held overnight by a stranger, how long would you have to keep her outside, unattended, for this to be statistically likely to happen?

About seven hundred and fifty thousand years.

But if we rarely heard about kidnapped children before the eighties (with the exception of the Lindbergh baby), they have since become a staple of TV. A particular child's story that captures the public's interest can go on for months—sometimes years. To this day, the JonBenet Ramsey case can still start an argument, even though the mother was exonerated and has gone to her grave. Between that case and Elizabeth Smart and Maddie McCann and Caylee Anthony, we all feel as if we "know" someone who disappeared. We've watched their home videos. We've "met" their families on TV. And because we've heard about them so much, their stories start to seem tragic, yes, but not totally surprising. They fit perfectly into a worldview that says, "Just another example of kids getting snatched and killed." Our brain has stored all the other stories before it, so each new one just confirms our belief that child abductions are happening all the time.

So now, when you're thinking about whether you could ever let your kids hang out by themselves in the video game department at Target—which is where we deposit ours, because otherwise they'd moan and groan the whole time we're trying to concentrate on various Mr. Coffee features—you automatically think about Adam Walsh snatched from the Sears. Even though that was in 1981. Even though, every day, millions of parents go shopping with their whiny kids, and the kids wander off for a while, and the parents panic and then they find them in the toy department and everyone's OK. It's hard to remember, but we should: the likelihood of something truly tragic happening is, thank God, extremely low.

Now let's look at how the folks in the TV biz work to make us feel otherwise.

"As a former TV news producer," a dad confessed in an e-mail to Free-Range Kids, "I can tell you that news is all *about* fear. Sometimes, the first criteria we used when judging a story involving children or families was, 'Is it scary enough?'"

When the answer was "no," that didn't necessarily kill the story. It just changed the way it was reported—and teased.

"A tease has to hit people in their heartstrings, where you know your words are going to have some impact: their personal safety, or the safety of their family," said another former TV news producer, Thomas Dodson. "It has to grab the viewers' attention, and you have a very short time to do it."

So instead of saying, "If your child is under age three and you happen to have shopped at that little toy store on Elm Street where the proprietor bought some funky wooden blocks from Finland, please note that these *could* pose a choking hazard if your kid put several of them in his mouth at once, which he probably wouldn't, since they taste bad," you would say (according to Dodson): "A massive recall of toys! Is something in your child's toy box on the list?"

(To which, by the way, a friend once remarked: "If something that terrible is out there, threatening my children, why the hell are they making me wait till eleven to find out?")

TV stations love those toy recalls because that way their newscast gets to scare people (good for ratings) while also doing a public service (good for the soul). It's like exposing OSHA violations at a strip club.

Now maybe there *is* some point to telling us the most anguishing stories of our day, every day. But I've been a reporter for twenty years, and I'm still not quite sure what that point is. Is it to warn us about a dangerous neighborhood? That's helpful, I guess. Or to remind people to look both ways when crossing the street or to drive safely? Can't overemphasize those. Is there an exploding rattle out there that we shouldn't buy? Tell all! But, as former Tucson anchorwoman Tina Naughton Powers says, "On local news, it's, 'Good evening and welcome to death, doom, and destruction. Here's what didn't happen to you today, but it could so we'll keep you in fear!'"

So when Anderson Cooper hosts an hour-long special on missing children, as he did in 2007, he never says, "First off, remember: this will probably never, ever, *ever* happen to you. In fact, it's almost ridiculous that I'm even here talking about it." No, he turns to the camera with those devastatingly earnest eyes and says, "It is every parent's nightmare."

Then he interviews the parents who lived that nightmare— their boy rode off on his bike, never to be seen again. Then he talks to a "safety expert" who talks about kids getting snatched from their bikes and calls it "a common scenario."

Common? It is so *not* common that it almost never happens. About twenty times more kids are killed by drowning—is that common? Forty times more are killed by car accidents. *Forty* for every kidnapped kid. But would you call a fatal car accident common? Tragic, yes. Common, no.

"Not a word about probability has been spoken," notes *The Science of Fear* author Gardner. "Having just seen a string of horrifying examples, [one might] conclude that the chances of this crime happening are high."

And, in fact, that's exactly what people do. "Aren't kids always getting pulled off their bicycles in the suburbs?" a city friend asked me last year. She was serious. And scared.

Night after night, a vision of the world comes into our living rooms and our lives that is sad, sadistic, and totally at odds with the odds. Turn it off and you'll probably be a little more at peace. A little less worried about your kids' safety.

That may sound like I'm saying, "Ignore the awful truth and go live in La-La Land." But I'm trying to say that that horror concentrated on the tube is a fake land of its own—Agh! Agh! Land. It's a soul-freezing, hope-crushing place. If you lived there, you'd be dead now.

Or at least impaled on a towel hook.

REAL WORLD

The First Thing I Did Was Disconnect the Cable

Writes a Free-Ranger:

> I have to say that I am an overprotective mother and have
> tried to loosen up a bit lately. I do not want my children to
> grow up in fear of everything. I am taking baby steps—just
> allowing my children, one being a teen, to go to the park
> across the street unsupervised—but I am getting there. The
> first thing I did was disconnect the cable. Not because of what
> the kids were watching but because of what I was watching.
> Just like the Internet. If something catches my eye, I read it.
> But if it is about another child abduction or another school
> shooting, I do not read it. I am trying to let go of those fears
> that the media has generated.

Going Free Range

Free-Range Baby Step: Don't
touch that dial! Get today's bad
news from a newspaper instead. Maybe it'll have comics, too.

Free-Range Brave Step: No more keeping CNN on as background noise. I know, it's nice to hear a voice. But the fear seeps in even when you think it doesn't. Switch to music.

One Giant Leap for Free-Range Kind: Get up and go out. Spend that hour you were going to watch *Law and Order* on a walk with the kids instead. Look around at all the unspeakable crimes not being committed. This is called the Real World. (Not to be confused with MTV's version, which is a crime all its own.)

Avoid Experts

Who Knew You Were Doing Everything Wrong?... Them!

Did you read *What to Expect When You're Expecting*? Of course you did. Or your spouse did. Everyone did. I did. I found it very helpful.

And horrible.

Like most advice out there for parents.

Helpful because when you're wondering if those gas pains are really contractions, it's there to give you a clue. (If a baby's head is emerging, it's not gas.) But even though at times the newest edition bends over backward to reassure moms-to-be that they should "lose the guilt," the basic premise of this book is that there's a right way and a wrong way to act when you're pregnant, and a whole lot of dilemmas and potential pitfalls along the way. Or, as the introduction to the fourth edition cheerfully proclaims, "More symptoms and more solutions than ever before."

That's good, because moms just weren't worried enough.

Let's take a glance at the twenty-nine pages on "eating well." (Not to be confused with the brand extension, *What to Eat When You're Expecting*—a whole book. By the time you're done reading it, the baby's in law school.) Naturally, the authors tell moms to try to eat a balanced diet. Fine. But then they go on to say that this isn't just a question of trying to eat a few more spinach salads and a little less Kahlúa cream pie. No, the writers ask moms to kindly remember that "Each bite during the day is an opportunity to feed that growing baby of yours healthy nutrients."

Not each meal. Not each day. *Each bite* has to be carefully considered if you're going to be doing the right thing by your child. So "Open wide, but think first."

What are the consequences of a single bite you don't "think first" about? Oh . . . maybe the slow class at school for junior. Maybe weight problems for life. Or worse. After all, eating the precise number of calories and nutrients suggested by the book offers "impressive benefits," including "better birthweight, improved brain development, reduced risk for certain birth defects. . . ."

Aieee!! If that doesn't make mama throw her baloney sandwich out the window, what will? On the other hand, if that mama cannot resist the fatty meat and gobbles that darn sandwich right down to the crust, she is left to feel that she's a horrible person. A lax, no-good, baby-damning baloney addict—at least compared to the will-of-steel baby mamas the *What to Expect* authors applaud. Even in the food chapter's little box about *not* feeling guilty, they jauntily say, "Lose the guilt, hold the deprivation, and allow yourself a treat every once in a while." A treat that will make "your tastebuds jump for joy." And what exactly would that fantastic treat be?

"A blueberry muffin."

Not even a cupcake. I guess frosting is the *What to Expect* equivalent of crack.

Now listen: on the one hand, it's hard to argue with a book that says pregnant women should be eating well. On the other hand, it's hard *not* to argue with a book that drives pregnant women crazy. "It tortures them and it tortures me," says Dr. Craig Bissinger of the book he dreads seeing his patients waddle in with. As an obstetrician who teaches at Mt. Sinai Hospital in New York City, this is the sum total of his dietary advice for expectant moms: "Just eat like you have your whole life, but eat a little more."

So much for the "each bite" advice—advice so picky and so extreme, it's bound to make any mom self-conscious. (Aren't the people who think about the consequences of *each bite* generally referred to as anorexics?) It is exactly that hyperconsciousness—the worry that at any second we could be doing something terribly wrong that will hurt our children forever or, alternatively, that any second is another opportunity to produce the perfect child if only we don't blow it—that is one of the reasons we're so worried about our parenting capabilities. Even before our kid is born!

After birth, of course, it never ends. Go to the parenting section of your library or bookstore—or maybe you're there right now (so buy this book already!). In front of you awaits a wall of "expert" advice so daunting, you may want to cry. Then again, maybe you're there because you're already crying because you think you're such a bad parent.

This is not the place to look for reassurance. It's not that there's no good advice to be found here. Dr. Spock is still calm and good. *Baby 411* seems nonalarmist—it does things like remind moms that even if they don't breastfeed, "your baby will be fine if he is formula fed." The books on child development can tune you in to why your toddler isn't taking your every helpful suggestion yet. ("Sweetheart, let's not climb on the eighteenth-century porcelain elephant.") And of course if your child has been given a diagnosis of something you want to read up on, it's great that these books are here.

But . . .

I went flipping randomly through a whole bunch of these books, and I guarantee that if you tried to follow the advice in even a chapter or two of some of them, you would fail or at least forget the million particulars that you're supposed to do. And then you'll feel bad. Examples?

The Happiest Toddler on the Block—ah yes, let's compete for whose kid is happier—teaches parents how to talk to their tantrumming tots. It is not enough to tell a child who is freaked out by a broken cracker in her snack, "It's OK! It's OK!" No, you must "Save your reassurance for after you respectfully reflect your child's feelings."

That's right, folks. There is a wrong way to calm your children down, and it's by reassuring them. So next time you're talking to your kid, don't do what comes naturally. Think hard about what an expert told you to do and *then* talk. Otherwise, you'll be doing it wrong.

What if you want to encourage good behavior in your child? Saying "Yay!" is no longer enough. *Happiest Toddler* suggests rewarding moppets "with a pen check mark on the back of their hands when they have done something good." At night, "count the checks and recall what he did to earn each one. He'll end his day feeling like a winner!"

I'm not quite sure why this activates my gag reflex, but it has something to do with the fact that we are hereby expected to notice, cheer, and physically record every wonderful little deed our kid does that day, and then repeat it back, like the king's vizier. "First, my Lord, you woke up and did proceed not to throw your binky across the room. Huzzah, huzzah. Then, my Lord, when it was time for the day's morning repast, you did splendidly wield your spoon like a big boy . . ."

Without that litany, would the king end his day feeling like a winner? Perhaps not. Do you want to raise a kid who needs to hear his accomplishments reiterated every night as he gazes at the physical record of his wonderfulness?

Just asking.

Then there are books telling us how to communicate with our kids—and not just basic advice like "Try not to yell very much." No, they tell you the exact words, like you're a bumbling amateur who needs a script to say the right thing. Some of these books read like they're giving advice on how to navigate a tricky job interview. So in a book with the really promising title *Am I a Normal Parent?* there's a whole section on how not to quash your child's will to live when he asks if you like the picture he drew.

"How do you respond?" asks the book. "One way to help your child trust your response would be to take a minute or so to really look at the drawing and then, instead of commenting on the final product, say something about the process. For example, you might say, 'I like the way you drew a black circle around the sun to make it stand out. I also like the red shirt on the boy in the picture. It reminds me of the shirt you wore to your last birthday party.' This will help your child feel like your response was not a lie or a brush-off, but an honest reflection of what you have seen."

So I guess "That's beautiful, hon!" makes them think we're total liars and the world is a stinking cesspool of phonies? Really—I can see where the author wants to help parents relate to kids, but it seems to me that the more worried we are about the ramifications of every remark we make, the more stilted we become. We are *not* relating to our kids as kids. We are relating to them as complicated cakes we have been given to make, and if we don't follow the recipe exactly—a recipe given to us in painstaking detail by an expert chef angling for a TV baking show—the whole thing will collapse.

That same book has a whole page about whether to tell your child the tooth fairy is hooey—a topic parents have grappled with ever since winged ladies roamed the earth. Why do we suddenly need an expert telling us how to broach this touchy subject? Or any subject? Or every subject? Including—let me rant for another paragraph or two—a whole tome on potty training?

The Potty Training Answer Book asks many of the questions you may or may not have been wondering about, including, "What books and videos should I choose for my child's potty library?"

Her what?

You know—a how-to library filled with picture books like *I Want My Potty*, *It's Potty Time*, and even, I kid you not, *What to Expect When You Use the Potty*. (Thankfully, not for pregnant women.) *The Potty Training Answer Book* lists a full *twenty* books you might want to get your child about the issue.

And six videos.

Is your child studying for an advanced degree in Potty Studies? Has she been invited to present the "Scatological Preschooler" lecture at Oxford? I got through a college course on twentieth-century

Russian history with less reading. But the *Answer Book* then suggests some "favorite potty training resources." Because twenty books and six videos are just *not* enough.

Simply bringing the kid into the bathroom and plopping her on the toilet is not an option anymore. And simply asking your friends, "What worked for you?" is now considered about as sensible as asking them, "How would *you* perform a triple bypass?" It's not that potty training is such a breeze—I know it's fraught with frustration, and, for the record, I did give my kids *Everyone Poops* and some picture book my sister sent me, so it's not like I braved it alone. But when an author starts telling you not only to read potty books aloud to your child but to "extend your child's favorite potty stories and songs into everyday play situations" and to "use hand puppets, finger puppets or spoon puppets to have a conversation about potty training" and also to "retell stories from books and videos while you are driving in the car or walking to the store" and then to make your kid his own "personal potty book" complete with PHOTOS OF HIM to "increase his self-awareness" so he can "reflect on the images," and on and *on*, and this whole one-hundred-plus-page volume is considered a sane and helpful reference book rather than the feverish ravings of a bibliophilic, paid-by-the-word, bathroom-crazed, puppet-pushing potty brain—clearly, we are depending way too much on experts who make us think we have to do way more than necessary to help and understand and ultimately save our kids.

Where did this bizarre reliance on these folks come from? And can we wean ourselves off of it?

Jillian Swartz, editor in chief of the online magazine *Family Groove*, believes it all started the same way the Food Network did, sort of.

"Every ten years or so," says Swartz, "a new, once-mundane job becomes deified. Think: Chefs in the nineties and handymen and home decorators in the two thousands." About twenty years or so ago, another lowly job suddenly became chic: motherhood. (And, to a lesser extent, fatherhood.) "With this," says Swartz, "came the fetishization of every last mother-loving detail of parenthood, and an ever-burgeoning breed of experts to propagate this often mind-numbing minutiae. Pile on top of that the rise of Citizen Media and all the (mis)information online and we're all just swimming aimlessly in the murky waters of child-rearing do's, don'ts, who's, what's, how's, when's, and why's."

The avalanche of expert advice—and nonexpert advice on nonetheless very enticing Web sites—undermines our belief that we are equipped with enough common sense to deal with most child-rearing issues. That battered confidence, in turn, leads us to look ever more desperately to the experts wherever we find them. At the library. In parenting magazines. On TV. Online. But a lot of those experts give advice so daunting and detailed and frankly nondoable (does anyone really want to spend the day retelling potty stories with the aid of a spoon puppet?) that we feel like failures.

Then when—surprise—our kids turn out *not* to be perfect, we know who's to blame. We are! If only we'd made one more pretend forest out of broccoli spears, our kid would be a veggie fiend. If only we'd put aside that deep-fried Oreo in our second trimester, she'd be in the gifted program at school. And if our child is cranky? Uncommunicative? Headed for five to ten years' hard labor? That just might be because we told her, "Look, sweetie, a broken cracker is not the end of the world!" instead of saying, "Oooh, your cracker broke. Sad sad sad sad sad!" and respectfully relating.

The experts told us what to do, and we screwed up.

So what's the alternative? Reading every book and article and trying to do absolutely all the stuff they recommend? (She asked rhetorically.) Or avoiding the experts entirely and perhaps missing out on some good advice?

Well, it's obviously somewhere in the middle, according to a bona fide expert expert, Dr. Stephen Barrett. Barrett is board chairman at Quackwatch, a nonprofit group that examines the health advice being given to the public and flags the information that is scientifically unproven—or just plain wrong.

If you're looking for answers and don't know where to turn, Barrett says, "Look for credentials." A book by the American College of Obstetricians, for instance, or a site run by the American Academy of Pediatrics. "I don't recommend that people use Google to search for health advice," Barrett adds, because so much of what pops up is wacky. (More on that in a sec.) "The Internet has made many people more visible. I'm not sure that when it comes to advice, this is helpful."

I'm not sure, either. That's why Barrett's other suggestion—"Ask your doctor"—seems obvious, but smart. If you have a whole *lot* of questions, then ask your doctor to recommend a reliable book.

But of course, plenty of parents don't trust any of the old "reliable" sources anymore. They're more ready to believe the ones who say, "Whatever you've heard is fine, isn't." So sometimes, even if there's reassuring news—such as that the FDA has determined that the chemicals in plastic baby bottles are not going to turn your boy into a girl—it's hard to hear that message because it's the nay-saying "experts" who get the attention and airtime. (Did I mention in the media chapter preceding this one: fear sells?) Our generation is remarkably receptive to skepticism because we grew up learning not to trust any company or institution that says, "Trust us—you can trust us."

Most of us came of age right alongside the consumer protection movement. As kids we learned that car companies knew about brake problems but hid them from the public, even as the cigarette manufacturers knew they were giving us cancer but pretended that they didn't. Understandably, we grew up pretty cynical.

But over the years, as we stopped trusting additives and preservatives and pesticides and saccharine and Western medicine and government and pretty much anything that wasn't an organic potato wrapped in a recycled paper bag from Whole Foods, some of us just threw up our hands and decided it was impossible to trust anything or anyone. (Except Oprah.) The minute we heard something new and nefarious about a time-honored product or practice, a whole lot of us were ready to embrace it. Shampoo gives you cancer? We *knew* it!

The Web can confirm these fears—and spawn new ones. Is your water safe? Your cereal? Your sandbox? But as Barrett points out (knowing full well he will sound like just another "establishment" source not to be trusted): most companies really do not try to sell us deadly or defective products. Even if they have no corporate conscience whatsoever, doing wrong is still not worth it to them, because if they harm a single child, they'll have to recall millions of products. Or millions of us will join a class-action suit. Either way, that will hurt their bottom line.

So we have a choice: we can trust the self-proclaimed experts warning us that our body wash is toxic—and by the way, so is everything else—or we can just be glad we're living in a highly regulated society that truly isn't teeming with killer products.

In 1946, Dr. Spock famously began his baby care book with these reassuring words: "Trust yourself. You know more than you think you do." The mantra of today's experts—"Trust us. There is *so* much you don't know"—seems designed to drive us mad.

To calm down, remember that the best child-rearing advice boils down to the old basics. Listen to your kids. Love them. Keep them out of oncoming traffic.

And when you're pregnant, don't eat a baloney sandwich in oncoming traffic, either.

REAL WORLD

Baby Magazine Madness

A Free-Ranger who signs herself, "Living in Fear" writes:

> I read some "advice" from a baby magazine saying that you should not leave the baby in the house and run out to get the mail—you never know when a fire may start. It's making me *crazy*.

Going Free Range

Free-Range Baby Step: Don't buy any new parenting books unless they have the words "Range" or "Free" somewhere in the title.

Free-Range Brave Step: Immediately stop Googling any and all combinations of the words "toxic," "childhood," "should," "esteem," "whole grain," "cover-up" and "guilt."

One Giant Leap for Free-Range Kind: Free yourself from advice overload by remembering that we got to this point in human history without the benefit of child-rearing manuals, pregnancy diet books, or potty training treatises. If you seek parenting advice, first try asking an older parent you admire. She'll be thrilled, and her advice won't last 378 pages.

Boycott Baby Knee Pads

And the Rest of the Kiddie Safety-Industrial Complex

The jazzy strains of the CBS *Early Show* theme song are coming from the living room. "Parents of any age are about to get something a little extra on Mondays," promises the pleasant host. "This morning we launch our weekly segment called 'Parental Guidance,' with a look at some potential dangers found in almost every home."

Help for us clueless parents. Hooray.

The show goes live to a Manhattan apartment where James Hirtenstein, a professional babyproofer—yes, it's a real job now—is perched at the top of a steep staircase. He is about to take us on a tour of all the scary parts of this apartment, though I promise you, if you're talking about a duplex in Manhattan, the scariest part must be the mortgage. Hirtenstein begins with the stairs, of course, recommending a special kind of gate. Then he goes to the living room, where he recommends little stoppers that keep the doors from shutting all the way, lest they chop off a child's finger. In the kitchen, he recommends locks on the fridge, lest a child . . . I'm not quite sure what. Grab a beer? And then he is ready to discuss perhaps the scariest room in the house.

"Bathroom!" he says. "Extremely dangerous." He's speaking in staccato now, like a Marine. "Toilet lid locks have to be on every toilet in the house!"

"Why?" asks the host.

"*Why?*" the babyproofer replies. "On average two children a week die in toilets."

Two a week? What a horrible way to go!

Some parents probably didn't even wait for the commercial before sprinting off to the babyproofing store—or sprinting off to call Mr. Hirtenstein's babyproofing company. But if they had sprinted off instead to the Web site run by the U.S. Consumer Product Safety Commission—the federal agency that warns us about everything from recalled baby swings to defective toasters—they could have looked up the actual statistics on death by toilet bowl drowning. And guess what?

"The typical scenario involves a child under three years old falling head first into the toilet," reads the agency's home drowning study. "CPSC has received reports of sixteen children under age five who drowned in toilets between 1996 and 1999."

Sixteen children over the course of four years. That's four a year.

Not two a week.

Of course, any drowning is a terrible tragedy. And little children do need to be supervised in the bathroom, and never left alone in the tub. (Read the Safe or Not? entry "Pools and Water and Kids and Toilets" to see why.) It is always a good idea to keep the bathroom door closed. *But* the babyproofer's stats were off by 2600 percent! The fear that he sowed in millions of viewers will now make them more certain than ever that their children are living in incredible danger.

Which works very nicely, if you happen to be in the biz of selling kid safety products to parents.

This is not say that all purveyors of these products are out to hoodwink parents. It's not even to say that there aren't some wonderful products out there that really do make children safer, like car seats, which have lowered the chances of a fatal car injury by over 50 percent. It's just to say that in order to sell $1.7 billion worth of products to parents and make raising a child an extremely pricey— not to mention nerve-racking—proposition, businesses have to convince parents that minor dangers are major. Which is exactly what has happened.

Let's take a look at some of the newer safety products being marketed to parents, starting with baby knee pads.

Yes, knee pads. Exactly what you'd want your nine-month-old to wear if he were drafted into the NFL. Except that these pads— "the cushiest, comfiest knee pads ever," according to the One Step Ahead catalog—are for crawling. "These medical-grade neoprene knee guards give little crawlers unparalleled protection, while slip-proof 'traction beads' guard against skidding."

Skidding? Like your baby is going to round the corner so fast, we'll see sparks shooting out of her Huggies? What kind of fools do they take us for, that we'd be worried about this time-honored stage of babyhood? Knees were *made* for crawling. So were kids! Yet look what one mom wrote on the One Step Ahead Web site, under the baby knee pads "product review."

"Sometimes my daughter has problems going from carpeting to the wood and marble floors. It helps her with traction to keep from spinning out. Unfortunately, she did not like the feel on her legs and refused to wear them."

Score one for the baby! But that mama—she really worries about her daughter "spinning out" while crawling. And other parents writing to the site were just as sold.

Another product you see advertised in parenting magazines lately is the "Thudguard"—a helmet to protect your child while he's engaged in that extreme sport known as toddling.

"It's about time that someone has addressed the diffuse head injuries that are . . . on the rise for toddlers learning to walk," wrote one doctor in an endorsement of the product.

Oh really? On the rise? Because suddenly evolution made a U-turn and now children are careening into walls and tables like never before?

And even if babies do bump and bumble, are they really in danger of sustaining serious "head trauma," as claims the ad for this $39 helmet (that makes your child look like he just had brain surgery)? Let us consult again with calm, wise Dr. F. Sessions Cole, chief medical officer at the St. Louis Children's Hospital.

"We see 65,000 to 70,000 patients a year," says Dr. Cole. "How many are associated with significant head trauma that resulted from instability as toddlers learned to walk?" he asks.

None.

That's a number that's not going up and not going down. Unlike sales of Thudguard, which was originally a British product but is now available in America and everywhere else parents are flipping out.

At the Babies R Us near me, there's an entire room devoted to child safety devices: unsurprising stuff like cabinet locks and electrical outlet covers. Ridiculous stuff like easy-to-grip baby soap. (Good in baby prison, I guess.) And then there's a whole display of special car mirrors that allow you to watch your baby in the backseat as you drive. "Why do you need one of these?" I asked a dad reaching for one.

"To see if the baby's OK," he said.

I suppose I knew he'd say that. But what we're talking about here is a parent checking up, while driving, on a child who is already strapped snugly into a federally approved car seat. A child strapped in there with a five-point belting system specifically to be "OK." It's really hard to imagine how the child would not be OK, and besides, if he were fussy, you'd hear him. Then, at a stoplight, you could turn your head and look at him.

But now, with about ten different special child car mirrors to choose from, it starts to feel as if good parents do have to check on their car-seat baby even more often. That means they have to take

their eyes off the road. And that's really too bad, because car accidents are the NUMBER ONE PREVENTABLE CAUSE OF CHILDREN'S
DEATH in America. Naturally, we don't know how many are caused
by parents taking their eyes off the road and peering into their baby
rearview mirrors. But as parents are always saying, better safe than
sorry.

Leave the mirror at the store, and the whole family will probably
be better off. And you'll save enough money for ice cream for everyone, too. (There is nothing dangerous about ice cream. Nothing.)

Here's one last example of a safety product that we don't need,
and how it undermines our own good sense: the heat-sensitive
bath mat.

This is a mat you put in the bottom of the tub. Turn the water
on, and if the words TOO HOT! magically appear in a bubble near
the duckie's head, you know that the water is, indeed, too hot! Because who can trust her own wrists anymore?

Oh wait a sec. We all can. Dip a wrist in the water, and you
yourself can tell if that water is warm, cold, or boiling hot. (Key
word: YEOW!) So why on earth is there not only this heat-sensitive
bath mat for sale but also a competing turtle you can put in your
tub that will indicate TOO HOT! too? (Not a real turtle, who would
indicate that by turning into soup.)

Why? Same reason you can buy a blanket with a headboard
built into it, in case you want to hold your baby but are worried
about breaking his neck. Forget the fact you have an arm built for
that job.

Same reason you can buy a harness to hold up your kid up like
a marionette while she learns to walk. Forget the fact you could
hold her up yourself, or even let her fall. She's got a bottom built
for that job.

In fact, forget the fact that three hundred thousand years of
evolution have made human children pretty sturdy and parents
pretty competent at raising them. We have entered an era that says
you cannot trust yourself. Trust a product instead.

It's hard to pop outside this snow globe of fear and gaze down on it objectively, but for Susan Linn, a mother and stepmom, that happened when she went to Chile to adopt her baby.

"I live in Brookline, Massachusetts, where everybody wants to do the very best for their children," says the Harvard psychologist. "So I was obsessing about crib bumpers and what are the best kind blah, blah, blah and then I got down there and she was in this teeny, tiny doll's crib and she was doing just fine."

So what kind of bumpers did Linn eventually buy?

"We never got them. It just didn't make any sense. She had a wooden crib, and if she banged her head, it wasn't going to hurt." And now that little girl is twenty-something and just fine.

Linn went on to found the Campaign for a Commercial-Free Childhood. Its goal is to get companies to quit marketing stuff to kids (good luck), while also trying to counter all the marketing aimed at parents. She's especially miffed by the marketing that tells parents their children need educational toys to get ahead.

"The message that parents are getting from birth is that they need these things to be good parents," says Linn. She adds: "They don't."

It was her organization that forced the Baby Einstein people to drop the word "educational" from their marketing materials and refund customers' money. "Because there's no credible evidence that baby videos are, in fact, educational for babies," says Linn. "The American Academy of Pediatrics recommends *no* screen time for children under two."

So forget the idea that a child learns best by watching TV— even if the soundtrack is by Mozart. When they're glued to a DVD, no matter how PBS-approved, they are not doing the one thing that really has been proven to enrich them and stimulate their neurons: *interacting with the world*.

Linn's current bugaboo is the Einstein line extension, Baby Neptune, which promises to teach children all about water.

"Within a baby's first year of life, new experiences can transform what might otherwise seem to be ordinary events into exciting opportunities for imaginative play," claims the Baby Neptune blurb. "Baby Neptune exposes little ones to the wonders of water in their world—whether they're stomping in the rain, splashing in the bathtub, playing 'catch me if you can' with the tide on the beach. . . ."

Stop! Oh please, stop! First of all, the idea that "within a baby's first year of life" a baby is already bored with "ordinary events" is ludicrous. How can babies be jaded about ordinary events? Nothing is ordinary to them yet! If it were, they wouldn't find their toes so endlessly fascinating. Or those black-and-white mobiles. Or their spit.

Second, the blurb talks about "exciting opportunities for imaginative play." But where, precisely, is the imaginative play in watching TV? If you want your kids to learn all the wonders of "stomping in the rain" and "splashing in the bathtub"—put them there! Water is not difficult to find. Let them feel it and taste it and enjoy it, not just stare at some other kid frolicking on a $14.99 DVD!

Okay. I'll calm down. Point is: educational baby media products are brilliantly marketed and utterly unnecessary. But even if you don't buy into them, they reinforce the idea that babies need to start their "education" right away. Sometimes even in utero. (You've heard of those tapes, right, that you play to the fetus? Or at least aim at your belly button?)

Now if all these videos were just marketed truthfully: "Here's something for your kids to watch while you answer your e-mails and then start mindlessly browsing the Web. It won't make them any smarter, and it may make them cranky when you turn it off, but it's not the end of the world if they watch it, either"—*that*, at least, would be fair. It doesn't promise us too much; it doesn't damn us too much, either. But best of all, it wouldn't make us so confused about what is "best" for our children and what isn't. Otherwise, it's really hard to tell, because it seems that lately every possible toy or class or activity or event or show or utter piece of junk is peddled to us as "educational." (Though once in a while, someone may substitute "stimulates creativity.") This is not only bamboozling; it also leads us to assume we're supposed to spend every second of the day pumping our kids full of brilliance. Another thing to worry about.

This educational obsession can take an ordinary toy—like a little battery-operated light-up drum I saw the other day—and instead of labeling it, "Loud, annoying thing," insist that it is actually a developmental showstopper: "Promotes hand-eye coordination!"

That it does. Promotes finger-in-ear coordination, too.

A package of foam rubber letters to play with in the tub said, "Inspires imagination"—as if the kid were going to start composing Moby-Dick above the soap dish.

Meantime, an article in one of the parenting magazines, "Why Music Boosts Brainpower," begs the question: If music didn't boost brainpower, would it be worthless? In the eyes of a society bent on producing wunderkinds, maybe so. (Another article said cuddling may boost babies' IQs. That's good, because otherwise we certainly wouldn't bother cuddling the helpless blobs, right?)

The music article went on to give all sorts of suggestions as to how to make your child more musical, while cheerily noting, "Raising a music lover is easy. If you start early and keep it fun, your child won't miss a beat."

God help those who don't start early. (Never mind that George Gershwin didn't even have a piano in his house till he was twelve—one of my favorite anecdotes.)

So we sign our kids up for Gymboree or Kindermusik, or maybe we take them to the local class on "sound and movement" like I did with my older son—a class so boring that the other nannies and moms looked ready to cry. The kids already were. After one of the sessions, I bolted out with another mom, and we bonded by confessing, "God I hate going there!" But go we did, because we didn't want our children to end up nonmusical. (Even though mine did. And last year we gave him private electric guitar lessons he didn't really like, either.)

There is nothing wrong with exposing your children to all sorts of opportunities and toys, of course. But there's nothing wrong with scaling back a little, either, even on the educational and safety product front. I know the catalogs keep coming, and other parents show up with all the latest inventions, but now is the time to try resisting some of that "You need this thing to make your kid safe, smart, and happy" drumbeat. The one beaten on that oh-so-educational, battery-operated drum.

Enrichment is all around us. Danger is not. Keep those two straight, and your family will be richer in every sense of the word.

REAL WORLD

"Baby Whatever" Videos—What a Freaking Scam!

A Massachusetts mom writes:

> I remember when my kids were babies, I had never really heard of the Baby Whatever videos. One of my friends raved and raved about them. I happened to see one at this friend's house once and thought, "This? That's it? This is the most boring useless drivel I have ever seen. What a freaking scam!" So I never ever purchased one. Instead, I let my kids play with toys, pull pots and pans out of the cabinet, bounce in their Exersaucer, and other such things.
>
> My favorite Baby Einstein video story was at a playgroup once. The playgroup met at another mom's house. She was another Baby video junkie. She put on a video, and the babies, who were about 9–11 months old, stopped playing with their toys and crawling around and just sat and stared. Except for my son. He first tried to crawl behind the TV to see what was there. Then he went over to one of the mesmerized kids, looked at the kid, looked at the TV, and took the other kid's toy.
>
> That's my boy!

Going Free Range

Free-Range Baby Step: Walk through the baby safety department of a store with your oldest living relative asking, "Which of these things did you need?"

Free-Range Brave Step: Your choice: try a day without baby videos or a day without table bumpers. See if your child has learned something new (perhaps the hard way) by day's end.

One Giant Leap for Free-Range Kind: Do something that will truly make your child safer and does not involve any new, dumb doodads: test your smoke alarm. Make sure it has working batteries. Make a deal with yourself to change them twice a year, when you change your clocks.

Don't Think Like a Lawyer

Some Risks Are Worth It

Every year, the fifth graders at my sons' grammar school go on an overnight to a nature preserve. A few weeks beforehand, the parents gather in the school's lunchroom to hear details of what to pack and what the kids will be doing.

"... rain poncho, hat, water bottle, bug repellent ..." Gary, the assistant principal, is reading from a list. He has been reading for a while. "... sun block, flashlight, antibacterial wipes ..."

"I know you're CPR certified," says a mom, raising her hand, "but are there other teachers who are?"

Another mom raises her hand. "Do the kids have to go on *both* hikes?"

And a dad: "Are we going to get a contact number?"

Gary answers yes to all three, though when pressed he admits that the contact number only rings the front office of the nature preserve. This upsets the dad who wants all the chaperones to carry cell phones he can reach at any moment. Another parent asks about the proximity of an emergency room. Finally Gary steers the discussion back to the trip and unveils the most exciting part of all: "At night, there's going to be a campfire!"

A room's worth of eyebrows shoot straight up.

"I just want to assure everybody that the kids sit twenty-five feet away," he says quickly.

Eyebrows wiggle uncertainly.

"There will be a row of benches in front of them," Gary adds. "Between the kids and the fire."

He gives a pleading smile, and most of the eyebrows back hesitantly down, as parents try to erase their mental pictures of little Jenna or Jeremy going the way of Joan of Arc. Deftly, Gary changes the subject to what food will be served. Wisely, he does not mention anything flambé.

And so it goes, in an era when any time children are about to venture outside the home or classroom, adult minds fly straight to thoughts of *What terrible thing could possibly happen?* to *If it does, are we prepared?* to *Watch out or we'll see you in court.* No wonder *The Worst-Case Scenario Survival Handbook* is such a best-seller. We are "worst case" parents, worrying all the time, right down to picturing the legal battle we'll pitch if we don't get what we want or if our kids don't, or even if, heaven forbid, a tongue tip gets scorched by a smoldering s'more.

Sure it makes sense to think ahead, and some activities really are dangerous. That's why whenever you go sailing, you wear a life vest. When you go skydiving, you wear a parachute. When you go for a motorcycle ride, you wear a helmet. (And if you are my child and reading this: you *never* ride a motorcycle. Hear that? NEVER.)

What has changed over the past generation or so is that now people worry like that about *every* activity, even ones that used to be considered simple and pleasant. Sitting around a campfire. Playing a game of ball. Even walking home from school has joined the list. Parents feel they must be super prepared for the worst of the worst, or else they're being irresponsible. Let's go to the suburbs to see how this plays out.

My friend's husband—we'll call him Hank—used to be a high-powered lawyer in the city. Now he's a stay-at-home dad in the 'burbs. Think of the implications. Law. Kids. Time. Naturally, Hank is on the School Bus Safety Committee at his eight-year-old daughters' school. And naturally, they're twins.

So what does Hank teach the tots in his safety program? In fact, what does he reteach them every year they are in grammar school?

"Get on the bus, sit down fast, buckle your seat belts, and pipe down," he says. Which sounds perfectly cool, if slightly urgent. "And we tell them to make sure their backpacks aren't fastened at the waist."

What?

"You know how some backpacks have those belts around the waist that you can fasten? We want to make sure theirs aren't."

"Why?"

"Well, just in case they're getting off the bus and the bus driver isn't paying attention and he closes the door too fast and their backpack gets caught inside and they're outside and they can't unfasten their belt and he doesn't hear their screams, so they get dragged down the highway a mile or two before anybody notices."

"My God!" I stare slack-jawed at Hank. "Has that ever happened?"

"Well, not that I know of. But . . ."

Just. In. Case.

Now, the hard thing about arguing against the Just in Case mentality is that once you can picture an eight-year-old (or her twin) being dragged down the street by her Hannah Montana backpack while the bus driver digs Zeppelin on his cranked-up, off-brand iPod, it certainly seems worth warning the kids to undo their backpack belts. It's so simple. And then—whew! That's one worry off the checklist.

The problem is, the checklist just keeps growing. It's like those brooms in the story of the sorcerer's apprentice. Chop one in half, and it comes back as two. Two become four.

Worries multiply because we are an imaginative species, and parents are more imaginative than anyone else, at least when it comes to envisioning the wide-screen, Dolby-sound worst. But our worries also get a big boost from professionals: lawyers, principals, and politicians who get a lot of bang for the buck by appearing extremely concerned about our children's welfare. They're all imagining the worst-case scenario, too. And the result is a lot of people so busy preparing for the hideous and unpredictable future that they think nothing of trampling the safe and happy present.

Thus nature centers make kids sit so far from the bonfire that they might as well be home watching that six-minute Yule log video loop that local TV stations play for hours every Christmas. Meanwhile, schools ban activities. Parks ban games. The Chicago suburb where my sister-in-law lives doesn't allow anyone to play baseball on the local ball fields unless they obtain a permit. So, legally, kids cannot just drop by and play ball.

As the school year began in another suburb of Chicago, one grammar school's teachers were required to sit their students down and impress upon them the dangers of . . . hula hoops. The kids were told not to swing the hoops around their necks or arms or *roll them around the playground*.

I am trying really hard to imagine how a rolling plastic hoop could possibly hurt anyone except, perhaps, an ant in the wrong place at the wrong time. But for ants, a playground is always the wrong place, and recess is always the wrong time.

Apparently it's always the wrong place and time for kids now, too.

"Something like 40 percent of schools have gotten rid of recess," says Philip Howard, chairman of the bipartisan legal reform group, Common Good. "Part of the reason is the obsession with testing and that every minute should be spent drilling for the test. But another reason is that you have to monitor recess, and there's liability." Schools are so afraid of being sued, they feel they have no choice but to protect themselves from lawyered-up parents, and the most efficient way to do that is to make sure students don't do anything where they could possibly injure themselves. Like roll a hoop. Or play.

That's why so few schools have those ropes we used to climb in gym. (Personal aside: yay. I never could get off the knot.) Some have cut out shop class, dances, and after-school sports. Plenty have outlawed dodgeball. (Personal aside: double yay! Who wants to get slammed with a ball? But my kids miss it.) An elementary school in Attleboro, Massachusetts, has gone so far as to outlaw the game of tag because, as the principal said, "accidents can happen." And in England, where for generations the kids played a game called "conkers"—you tie a horse chestnut to a string and try to break your friends' nuts (that really does sound bad)—that game has been all but outlawed, too. Or wait—that's not totally right. At some schools you *can* play it—if you wear goggles.

It's easy to laugh at those schools missing the big picture: most kids not only survive recess, they need it to survive the *rest* of the day. But the seemingly paranoid principals have a point, too: lose one lawsuit and, instead of buying pencils and paper, the whole school system could end up paying for someone's château in Provence. Besides, it's not as if the principals *like* being spoilsports (though it sure looks as if some of those playground monitors do). A nationwide survey of five thousand principals found that 20 percent of them spend five to ten hours a week writing reports or having meetings just in order to avoid litigation. Can you imagine what a drag that is? But they don't have much choice: half of all principals say they've already been threatened with a lawsuit. So hasta la vista, hula hoop. I'm sure the jump rope (don't strangle yourself!) is next.

This fear of lawsuits is having the same effect beyond the schoolyard. Normal childhood has become just too risky to permit. So while a Connecticut park district considers a ban on sledding, a parent sues Little League for not teaching her son the ins and outs of sliding. He broke his leg. Another parent sued an American Legion baseball team because the sun was in her child's eyes. Another mom sued a baseball league when she got hit by a ball that she said the coaches should have taught the player to catch. (The butterfingers was her own daughter.)

The people who run these activities have understandably become so fearful of financial ruin that they keep curtailing what's allowed. That's why I'll bet that even if your children were taught to swim somewhere, they were not taught how to dive. You may also live in a school district where students are no longer taught how to drive. And here's a little waiver you have to sign in California: "I fully understand my minor's participation may involve risk of serious injury or death."

That's to participate in a *piano recital.*

I could go on and on about how this fear of lawsuits results in even crazier stuff, like the warnings collected by Bob Dorigo Jones, president of the Michigan Lawsuit Abuse Watch. His organization runs the annual Wacky Warning Label Contest, which has produced such winners as "Remove child before folding." That was on a baby stroller. On a scooter: "This product moves when used." On an iron: "Never iron clothes while being worn." On a snowblower: "Do not use on roof." And on a box of birthday candles: "Do not use soft wax as ear plugs or for any other function that involves insertion into a body cavity."

Happy birthday to . . . ewww.

Anyway, you get the idea. I'll stop. (OK. One last label: "The Vanishing Fabric Marker should not be used as a writing instrument for signing checks or any legal documents.")

When companies feel compelled to issue warnings like these, it's not because they want to win some contest. It's because they actually do have to protect themselves from being sued for the weirdest, most ridiculous reasons. Reasons that you'd think would get tossed right out of court. "Your honor, I was simply trying to blow the snow off my roof . . ."

But sometimes a court does agree to hear a case like that, which is what drives Common Good's Howard crazy: "Allow lawsuits against reasonable behavior and pretty soon people no longer feel free to act reasonably." In other words, once a court allows a parent to sue Little League because her kid broke his leg sliding into second, Little League has no choice but to start thinking up ways to prevent all future sliding suits. Which means they just may decide to outlaw a time-honored, crucial part of baseball—the very sport they're trying to teach. It's nuts! But it's rational, too.

What's worst about this kind of defensive thinking is that eventually it seeps into our own parenting decisions. We start to wonder if it's OK to let our kids do anything, because . . . what if? What if they fall off their bike or the trampoline? What if they stay home alone and accidentally trip on a toy ? What if they walk home from the school bus stop and get hurt on the way? Is it our fault? The school's fault? The bus driver's fault?

Back in the 'burbs, Hank the bus safety dad has been thinking about that very issue. Although his town is so safe that the Clintons lived there when Hillary was a senator, school bus drivers are not allowed to drop kids off at the bus stop unless there is a responsible adult waiting to pick them up. (In other words: not Bubba.) If there's no responsible adult there? The driver has to turn around and drive the kid back to school. Someone there calls home, and someone from home has to come pick up the child.

Of course, school bus stops used to be considered a safe enough place to let off a kid. They were close enough to the kids' homes for them to walk—that was the whole point of a bus stop. But now even a two- or three-block walk is considered way too dangerous. An adult must be there, because . . . what if?

But here's another what if. What if we just let kids do the things we did as kids, like walk home from school or wait at the bus stop alone? Most of them would be perfectly fine. A few would get banged up. A very, very, very, *very* few might end up badly hurt— just as they did in our day.

That very, very, very, *very* small chance is one we're not willing to take anymore, in part because we know that in a court of law, a jury would probably find someone or something guilty. Schools don't want it to be them. Towns don't want it to be them. Companies don't want it to be them. And we parents don't want it to be us, either. So—thinking like lawyers—we cut out the dodgeball, the hula hoops, the sliding, the sledding, the walking, and, while we're at it, the warmth of the campfire, too.

The TV Yule log is still there if a kid really wants to watch. Provided he's properly supervised, of course.

REAL WORLD

Three Bumps in Two Years Is Not a Rash of Injuries

A Free-Ranger writes:

One mom sent an e-mail around to a bunch of other parents, saying that, "We need to get the school to remove the parallel bars in the playground. They are right at head level. In the past two years I have seen three kids run into them, and one needed stitches. This is too dangerous . . ." And on and on.

I wrote back to her (and cc'd the principal) saying: "There are over 700 kids at this school. Three bumps in two years is not a rash of injuries. Accidents happen. If we start taking everything out that someone might get hurt on, there will be nothing left. Some kids (like mine) are short, and cannot reach the higher parallel bars, and would like to be able to play on the playground as well."

She responded with some, "We'll have to agree to disagree" line. But I wanted her, and the principal, to know that not every parent thinks this way, and maybe she is over-reacting. I'm not sure if I made any headway with her, but I won't stay silent while the paranoid moms bubblewrap my kids' childhood.

Going Free Range

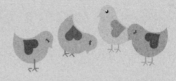

Free-Range Baby Step: Find a playground that has not been safety-retrofitted. OK, you may have to go to a Third World country (or, as we did, rural New York), but look for one with a merry-go-round or teeter-totter or even one of those now verboten horsie swings and let your kid have some prehistoric, possibly illegal fun. Feel free to ride the horsies, too. Just don't sue if you fall off.

Free-Range Brave Step: Try a whole day of not being prepared. Don't bring Kleenex, wipes, Band-Aids, water, a phone, or even extra cash. This may sound extreme, but once you muddle through, you'll probably feel a little more free. The world is not that threatening. You don't always have to be ready for the worst. When you think like a lawyer and imagine everything that could go wrong, it gets to be a habit. Try a day of kicking it.

Giant Leap for Free-Range Kind: Read the Real World box above this one and do what that Free-Ranger did. When your school or scout troop or park district proposes getting rid of a time-honored kid thing, gather some statistics and fight back. It's worth it.

Ignore the Blamers

They Don't Know Your Kid Like You Do

"Can you *believe* she did that?"

Melissa, my upstairs neighbor, is staring wide-eyed, the way you do when you want someone else to open her eyes equally wide and shake her head in disbelief, so the two of you can sit there bonding over your utter shock.

I am having trouble doing this.

"Well . . . it . . . it doesn't seem so bad," I venture, squinting apologetically.

"Lenore! I could have taken her baby, and she would never have seen him again! She was crazy!"

Ah, the crazy wars again. Who's crazy: people who trust other people, or people who don't?

In this case, I have to say that Melissa was officially crazy. Because the person she did not trust was . . . herself. Here's the story.

She—Melissa—was waiting in the checkout line at Costco, the giant warehouse store, with her groceries and her daughters, ages two and five. The woman in front of her suddenly remembered she had to get something at the back of the store and asked Melissa if she'd mind watching her baby, who was in the shopping cart. Melissa said fine, and off the woman, a stranger, sprinted.

She came back two minutes later to discover that Melissa had kidnapped and killed her baby.

No, no! Come on. Obviously, that's not what happened. She came back two minutes later, thanked Melissa, and that was that. One mom helping another. But even if that's how the other lady saw it, that's not what Melissa saw. She saw a wildly irresponsible woman entrusting her precious little boy to a total stranger who could have easily turned out to be a psycho killer buying bulk paper towels and Goldfish crackers—John Wayne Gacy in a dress.

All of which is a pretty harsh assessment of that mom's actions. First of all, the baby-mom did not choose just anyone. She chose another mom. One who probably would have had a pretty hard time yanking the boy out of his cart, abandoning her groceries (and place in line!), dragging him out of the store, dragging her *own* kids out of the store, remembering where she'd parked, unlocking the car, shoving everyone inside, strapping them into their car seats, and then gunning across the border, all while ignoring her little girls shrieking, "Mommy! Why are you stealing that lady's baby?" and "We want our Goldfish!"

Oh, and second of all, no one else would have noticed this little drama and perhaps said, "Uh . . . stop"?

This eagerness to distrust each other and even to find glaring fault with each other means that it's hard for moms and dads to relax, ever. If the only good parent is a parent who never leaves their kid's side—not even to run to the back of the store for a can of tuna fish—then it's very easy to spot the bad ones. They're the ones who let their kids walk to school or stay home alone for an hour. They're the ones inside while their kids play in the yard. They're the ones making their teenagers get themselves to their activities, or even their jobs. Things that previous generations did without a moment's hesitation—or tragic outcome—have become grist for the gossip mill.

"I let my eight- and ten-year-old sons bike the three blocks to a friend's house," a mom named Amy wrote to the Free-Range Kids blog. "But when they returned, their friend's mom insisted on accompanying them back home through our very safe neighborhood, 'just in case.'" The lady was sending Amy a message: your mothering leaves something to be desired.

Sometimes the message is even more direct. A woman named Jess wrote that now that she lets her fifth-grade son walk the five blocks to school—with a friend—her neighbor won't let her children play at Jess's house anymore. To this neighbor, says Jess, "I am a bad mother. I try not to let it get to me, I think I am anything but. I love my children and, like all mothers, only want the best for them." But Jess's definition of "the best" includes sometimes untying the apron strings. Other mothers find that tantamount to child abuse.

In fact, that's the very term they sometimes use.

Thirty-five-year-old Kelly McGovern is the mother of four boys and, she admits, a yard-sale junkie. She and her husband spend plenty of Saturday mornings hitting the sales in their Phoenix suburb, and one morning when they were just about to do that, their oldest son, age nine, said he felt a little headachy and didn't want to go.

"We'd never really left him before because you're always so terrified," says Kelly. "You hear these stories that if you even leave your kid in the car for two minutes, the police are on your case and the other moms will eat you alive." Could they possibly leave their boy on the couch for an hour or two, watching a Harry Potter movie?

"My husband and I said well, we got the smoke alarm. We got a house alarm we keep on all the time in case of the boogey man. My son's so responsible, he's not going to cook, he's not going to light a match. We told him don't eat anything, because heaven forbid you choke. We left him with the cell phone and the regular phone and we said, 'We'll call you every thirty minutes.'" And then—off they went.

At the first garage sale, they ran into an older acquaintance who asked, "Where's your other son?"

"Don't tell anybody—he's home," Kelly confided.

The older woman chuckled. "I had to do that all the time," she said. "That's the only way I could work."

A few weeks later, Kelly finally got up the guts to confide in friends her own age, the moms in her son's playgroup. "We were just yakking," says Kelly. "And I said, 'I left Mark home the other day,' and the other moms were like, 'You left him ALONE?' One mother said, 'What if a fire had started in the house?' I said, 'We have a smoke alarm. I assume he'd run out.' And she said, 'Someone could have broken in!' And I said well, we have a house alarm and we left him with two phones. And she threw her head back and raised her eyebrows and said, 'Well, SOMETHING could have happened! You could get in trouble! That's *illegal!*'"

Not one mom spoke up in Kelly's defense. So allow me. Very few states—as far as I could tell, only Illinois and Maryland, in fact—have laws that specify the age at which a child can be left at home alone. In Maryland, it's eight. In Illinois, it's thirteen—with the caveat that this is only applicable in cases where the adult left the youngster for an "unreasonable" period of time "without regard for the mental or physical health, safety or welfare of that minor." Leaving a kid on a couch with a burglar alarm, smoke alarm, and his parents on speed dial just does not sound like "without regard" for his safety.

Other states and cities have guidelines—not laws—mentioning ages ranging from nine to twelve. But what these guidelines note is that the issue is not whether a child is left alone, or even what age, but under what circumstances. If, for instance, the child left alone has a disability, that's clearly wrong. If he's fine but left without a way to call a caregiver or without food or heat, or left in any way that suggests abandonment or utter neglect—all that is not only appalling but also probably actionable. But all those scenarios are also very different from being left alone with a Harry Potter video and a plea to temporarily hold off on the Doritos.

Those differences—not too subtle—are lost on a legion of parents dying to win the "I'm a better parent" game. They play fast and hard by dreaming up all sorts of scenarios in which the other parent would have a big comeuppance, a disaster about which the blamers could smugly tsk, "I warned you, but you wouldn't listen."

And we get so used to hearing their wild what-ifs and did-you-ever-think-abouts that these start to sound almost reasonable.

So when that playgroup mom says, "What if a burglar broke in?" no one else in the group says, "Hang on a sec! We're talking about a Saturday morning in the suburbs. That's not really burglary prime time." And when the accusing mom says, "Fire! What about a fire?" No one is ready to chime in with, "Fires are rare. Not that they don't happen, but we all know Kelly's son. He's not the type to light cherry bombs in the basement or stand still and watch the furniture go up in flames without running out of the house. And while we're at it, most homes do not spontaneously combust." No, these moms kept letting the other one grope around for some fear—any fear—to win her point: I'm responsible and you're not!

Fear, no matter how far-fetched, usually does win. It wins because there's no way to totally discount it. Just because your house didn't burn down doesn't mean it *couldn't* have. And fear wins because it is also very powerful. Once you picture coming home to a charred Harry Potter fan, it's hard to shrug your shoulders. The problem is, if you picture the very worst outcome of every very safe endeavor, there is no way you can enjoy life. All you can do is smother it.

The playgroup moms' vote of no confidence shook Kelly to the core. For six months afterward, she didn't leave her son home alone again—even though she really believed he would be fine if she did. She was just too afraid of what her friends would say (or do) to her if they found out.

As it turns out, this is not an uncommon worry. Laurie Spoon, a mother of two in quiet Corinth, Mississippi, found herself frantically looking up the local laws on child abuse after her mother threatened to call child welfare on her. Laurie worried that she could end up being fined or even having her children taken away. What unconscionable abuse had she heaped on her sweet nine-year-old?

"I let her and this other little girl go to the movies," says Laurie, twenty-seven. "It was a matinee of *Nim's Island*. It's a G-rated kid's movie. I walked them inside the door—I didn't just drop them outside. It was a middle of a Saturday and they got their popcorn and stuff and I told them: when it's over, stay there, I'll come back and pick you up. Don't go outside the building." And that's exactly what happened. The girls ate their popcorn, saw the movie, waited to be picked up, and went back home.

When Laurie's mom found out, she was livid. Laurie had put those girls in peril! And it wasn't just grandma who was ready to call the authorities. "I have met a lot of other parents and they are appalled that I would let my child go to the movie theater, or get dropped off at Skateworld," says Laurie. When she finally found the child welfare statutes, Laurie discovered that the law is on her side. It's just other parents who are not.

I'm sure these shamers and blamers probably meant the best. Most of them, anyway. But they are holding their fellow parents to an almost impossible standard—constant supervision—that also just happens to be an unthinking, unyielding standard. Even if *you* know your child is capable of sitting on the couch for an hour, or sitting in a matinee and staying alive, there are many who still insist, "We know better! That's dangerous!"

And the threats they hold out—blame, ridicule, calling the authorities—leave a lot of us unable to trust our own instincts or even to show our children that we trust *them*.

And then there is that one other threat that is forcing us to reconsider every Free-Range impulse. The threat that wears suspenders. Or, as a friend once put it when we were discussing whether or not to let our preteens travel on their own: "I don't want to be the one on Larry King."

What he meant was, he's afraid of being blamed on TV, if something dreadful ever befalls his daughter.

That fear is so powerful, it prowls behind all the others. It makes us second-guess any parental decision, because we know that public suspicion and even infamy await any of us whose child is hurt.

When it comes to other types of tragedy, we are a lot more forgiving. We have come a long and admirable way from the days when we blamed the victim. Back then, when, for example, a woman was raped, we'd say, "She asked for it. Look at that short skirt she was wearing!"

But over the past generation or two, we came to understand that the real impulse behind that reaction was our own fear. If we could blame the victim for her fate, we could feel safe (and smug). All we had to do was convince ourselves that she did something we would never do. "*She* wears short skirts. *She* walks home through the wrong neighborhood. *She* is someone bad things could happen to. Not me. I'm different. So I'm safe."

That was a nasty way to think, and it's great we've moved beyond it. But if we have stopped blaming victims, we have totally reversed ourselves on another group: victims' parents.

The people we used to automatically mourn with when tragedy struck.

Now, when, say, a four-year-old is stolen from a hotel room where she was sleeping while her parents dined nearby—an activity that 99.9999999 times out of 100 would not result in headlines—those parents are in for it. "They should be thrown in prison!" railed a typical radio talk show host. Sympathy? Empathy? Forget it. The impulse is to hate and to blame. *They* were bad. *They* deserved it. This is what happens when you're an irresponsible parent!

"My niece broke her arm and the first thing all the other moms wanted to know was, 'Where was her mother?'" recalls Jen Singer, creator of MommaSaid.net. Those women wanted to be able to blame the mom for her negligence.

Unfortunately for them—I guess—the mother had been five feet away, and her girl just happened to fall off her swing. Bad things happen to the children of good parents. This is so hard to accept—harsh, fickle fate is so hard to accept in an age when we believe we can control everything—that we cast desperately about for someone to blame.

Blame and fear are like Mean Girls. They pal around together and make everyone else feel dumb and self-conscious, or at least like they're going to end up eating alone in the lunchroom if they don't suck up. In the movie *Mean Girls*, Lindsay Lohan gets her groove back by—what else?—believing in herself. And in her family and friends.

That may be a totally predictable Hollywood ending, but it's what we have to do, too. Believe in ourselves and our kids and even in the other parents who *would* be on our side if they weren't so scared. You can't live your life worrying about what the Mean Girls are going to say.

Or the shaming, blaming playgroup ladies, either.

REAL WORLD

My Son Was Picked up by the Cops

A Free-Ranger fumes:

> My 14-year-old son and his friends were picked up by the cops at the train tracks near our house because it is now so uncommon for kids to be out on their own that clearly they were up to something awfully suspicious by picking those blackberries that grow in profusion there. None of them had cell phone umbilical cords, so they were treated like drug-dealing runaway truant thugs! They were each individually delivered to their doorsteps in the police cruiser. As a result, my 8-year-old carries a note in his back pocket that says:
>
> > My mom knows where I am. She told me it was okay to be here and she knows I can get home on my own. If you really don't believe me, call her.
>
> And then there is our number. And then I've signed it. This may seem silly, but so far three different parents have called me while he's been out at the park near our house to make sure.

Going Free Range

Free-Range Baby Step: When you're about to remind a mom or dad about some extremely unlikely danger their child might face—a danger they are probably just as aware of as you are—hush.

Free-Range Brave Step: Volunteer to watch the kids who are waiting with your own kid for soccer to start or school to open—whatever. Explain to the other parents that you're offering them a little free time.

If they say no thanks, ask them to watch *your* kid.

One Giant Leap for Free-Range Kind: The next time you make a parenting decision that you're worried other moms or dads might find lax, see if you can get up the courage to tell them about it. Admit that you left your daughter home alone while you went grocery shopping. Admit you sent your young son out on an errand. Talk about these things so that other parents can open up, too.

The scary part, of course, is that they may jump on you. Hell hath no fury like a self-righteous parent. But it's also possible that at least some of them do the same things you do—or would like to—and have been feeling very uneasy about it. Now you've got a support team.

Blamers thrive on shame. Take away their power. Do not be ashamed of making parenting choices based on who your kid is, rather than on what the neighbors will say. Why are they talking about you anyway?

Eat Chocolate

Give Halloween Back to the Trick-or-Treaters

Halloween really needs another name. How about World's Stupidest Warnings Day? Does that work for you? It will if you ever look at any tips on how to have a "safe" Halloween.

One of my favorite warnings, reprinted on many Web sites including Halloween-Safety.com, tells parents, "Make sure, if your child is carrying a prop, such as a scythe, butcher knife or pitchfork, that the tips are smooth and flexible enough to not cause an injury if fallen on."

Fallen on?

Ding dong. Trick or—HELP! I've fallen right on top of on my plastic butcher knife prop—how do you like that? Darn its non-rubber-tipped sharpness, it is slicing straight through my sternum! Why oh why didn't my mother heed that advice on the helpful Web site that just happens to be sponsored by a Halloween supply shop and buy a smooth and flexible butcher knife (or pitchfork or scythe) instead?

I have just one question for the folks who dream up those safety warnings: Have you *ever* seen a knife land blade-side up?

But that's Halloween for you. A chance to be afraid of absolutely everything . . . if you're a parent. I'm so old, I remember back when it was a holiday that was supposed to scare the *kids*.

Halloween is just the perfect example of how a fun, even revered, childhood activity has been turned into an orgy of worrying, warning, spending, obsessing, and all-out fun-bludgeoning, thanks to a gaggle of forces thick as boiled eyeballs in Cup-of-Newt Soup.

The biggest fear on Halloween, of course, is that somehow, your nice, quiet neighbors—the ones you never got to know but somehow managed to live next to in peace and harmony the other 364 days of the year—have been waiting, like kids for Christmas, for this one day to murder local children. Murdering them on another day just wouldn't be satisfying, I guess, which is why they've shown such remarkable restraint. But a child homicide on Halloween—it just feels right.

They will kill your moppet by poisoning the candy they give out, obviously. Or by baking big, homemade cookies laced with nefarious (but chocolaty-good) drugs. Or by sticking razor blades in the proverbial apple—because of course no one would ever notice a giant, dripping gash in an apple before they bit into it, right?

It is amazing how far-fetched most of these fears look upon reflection, yet there is *not one* bit of Halloween advice that doesn't warn against those very evils. Feed your kids a big "spooky" dinner before they go out, the magazines tell us, so they won't be tempted to eat any of the candy before they bring it home for inspection.

My God—has being even sickeningly full *ever* stopped a kid from stuffing himself even sicker with candy? And what kind of Halloween would it be—what kind of *kid* would it be—if no candy got eaten on the way? I'm just surprised no one has suggested bringing along a bag of dried organic figs, in case the giggling goblins want something good to gobble! (Sorry. Flashing back to my own feature-writing days when we had to make ridiculous tips sound fun.)

The problem is, if you blithely ignore all these warnings, *you*, the sane parent, will be the one considered cavalier to the point of reckless. Really—to publicize this book and the whole idea of out-of-control parental fears thing, I had a brainstorm: "Why don't I have my sons go trick-or-treating and then call all the news channels to come watch me let them eat a piece of unwrapped candy?"

Well, even I realized how that would make me look: "Mom Jailed for Jeopardizing Sons in Cheap Publicity Trick." Alternatively, "Child-Endangering Mom Inspires Mass Burning of Own Parenting Book."

And meanwhile, some reporter who bravely jumped in to snatch the candy away from my boys (and later ate it himself) would be the "hero" of the night, and we'd hear his story every year from then on in. And then everyone would buy *his* book, *Unwrapped: The True Story of a Halloween Hero*. And I wouldn't even be able to make my point, because everyone would figure that any mom who let her kids eat unwrapped candy is right up there with Cruella de Vil, so . . . I didn't do it. Heck, even *I* grew up being told not to eat candy that had been obviously unwrapped. But why? Was there ever really a rash of candy killings?

Joel Best, a professor of sociology and criminal justice at the University of Delaware, took it upon himself to find out. He studied crime reports from Halloween dating back as far as 1958, and guess exactly how many kids he found poisoned by a stranger's candy?

A hundred and five? A dozen? Well, one, at least?

"The bottom line is that I cannot find any evidence that any child has ever been killed or seriously hurt by a contaminated treat picked up in the course of trick-or-treating," says the professor. The fear is completely unfounded. Now, one time, in 1974, a Texas dad *did* kill his own son with a poisoned Pixie Stix. "He had taken out an insurance policy on his son's life shortly before Halloween, and I think that he probably did this on the theory that there were so many poison candy deaths, no one would ever suspect him," says Best. "In fact, he was very quickly tried and put to death long ago." That's Texas for you.

And then there was a time in 1970 when a five-year-old died from ingesting heroin. But it turns out that in that instance, the boy got into his uncle's stash and accidentally poisoned himself. Afterward, the family sprinkled heroin on some candy to make it look as if a stranger had done this hideous thing.

And, OK, there *was* one other time some kids were given poison on Halloween. "A woman in the 1960s was annoyed with children that she thought were too old to trick or treat, so she put ant poison in their bags," says Best. "But it was labeled, 'ANT POISON.' She probably thought it was funny. Until the police arrived."

So, despite this wacky woman (who made her intentions pretty clear), we now have zero recorded instances of death by strangers' candy. And yet look at all the things that have sprung up in response to this myth.

First and most obviously, we've killed the whole idea of, God forbid, baking treats for the local kids. Any cookie a kindly neighbor makes is going to be automatically dumped in the trash, so why bother? Ditto, most fruit. I'm not saying the candy companies concocted these scary rumors, but they sure aren't knocking them down.

Then we have the concerned but misguided authorities reinforcing the fears that shouldn't even exist. In 1995, for instance, no less a maven than Ann Landers warned her readers (basically, everyone in America who wasn't reading her twin sister, Dear Abby), "In recent years there have been reports of people with twisted minds putting razor blades and poison in taffy apples and Halloween candy."

Reports? None substantiated. Rumors? Yes indeed. Rumors like the ones she was spreading! And those rumors ended up actually changing the holiday. To this day, Nationwide Hospital in Columbus, Ohio—one of the biggest children's hospitals in the country—offers free x-rays of any Halloween candy a parent is worried about.

"To be honest, it's really fluoroscopy," said Pam Barber, the hospital's spokeswoman. "You dump it all out on a tray and actually pass it through the fluoroscope, and the technician is standing there, so it will pick up anything metal. So if somebody's rammed a nail or any kind of metal into a piece of candy, that will show up."

If the neighbors were trickier than that, however, there is little the hospital can do. "We hand out a disclaimer to parents," said Barber. "We want them to understand that, just like a traditional x-ray, [fluoroscopy] would not pick up if someone used a hypodermic needle and injected a drug into a piece of candy."

Isn't that a weird thought? That someone in Columbus would be injecting drugs into candy? It's the kind of thing that happens in horror movies, maybe, but it just has not happened in real life.

Yes, agreed Barber, "We've been very fortunate that we have never ever discovered anything questionable."

But that's not fortunate. "Fortunate" is when, luckily enough, something quite possible doesn't happen. It's *fortunate* when your dog knocks over the end table just after you moved your ant farm to the top of the TV. It's *fortunate* when you get to the deli counter just before the guy who is ordering twelve pounds of provolone, sliced thin, for his Provolone Pride party. But to think you're just—whew—strangely lucky that no mass murderer has yet struck in your town is really thinking about life in a whole different way. An "I'm Living in *Halloween: The Movie*" way.

Spokeswoman Barber was really surprised when I informed her that to the best of an expert's knowledge, no child in America had ever been poisoned by a stranger on Halloween. Being a nice, normal person, she was delighted to hear it. In fact, once she started thinking about it, she laughed. "My gosh, *our* parents didn't worry about that kind of stuff. Shoot! I can remember they would take us all over town." Her family went to different neighborhoods where they didn't even know anyone, and it was so fun, she said. "And now you just wouldn't consider doing that."

Maybe I would.

"Good for you!" she said. "It would be great to bring back some of those childhood joys." Which is exactly what we're trying to do here, right?

Now think about what this unfounded fear of fiends—the ones living quietly next door or in the next neighborhood—has done to the holiday. It's not just that a hundred kids a year have to wait to eat their candy till their parents send it through Nationwide Hospital's fluoroscopes. It's that millions of kids curtail their actual trick-or-treating—or at least their parents do.

"Here in central Ohio," Barber (a great source!) went on, "there's a number of churches and organizations that now have trick-or-treat parties so you can still have the candy being distributed, but it's through an organization you feel comfortable with. We've noticed a real growth in that kind of celebration of Halloween—where kids are not going door to door."

There's absolutely nothing wrong with parties. Love 'em. But the thing we're forgetting is: there's nothing wrong with going door to door either—and there's a lot that's even better about it. It's a way for kids to meet their neighbors. A way for them to be independent. A way for them to make the neighborhood *theirs*. And even a way for them to get silly and spooked out. That can't happen if they're not allowed outside.

What can happen if kids are stuck *inside*, "Monster Mash" blaring? Aw, you know exactly what: a marketing rush to fill the void left by the demise of an actual, old-fashioned, kid-directed activity.

Halloween is huge now—$5 billion huge. Stores are jammed with ugly decorations meant to pump back in the fun that's been drained out. How ugly do they get? Our dentist puts up a "Halloween wreath" made out of orange feathers and plastic vampire bats. It's a hybrid of Christmas, goth, and Liberace, more painful than any cavity. But once you bring the holiday inside, you do have to decorate, and dollars will be spent (on dreck).

Bring the holiday inside, and parents start hanging out, too. They watch the kids, they help them with their games. "Here, Timmy. Let me bob for that apple for you." It's just like school all over again—except with parents instead of teachers, and punch instead of milk.

Some grown-ups even dictate costume choices. Many Halloween parties at schools and community centers now come with the caveat, "No scary costumes, please." For God's sake, isn't scaring kids the *point* of the holiday? Or at least a big part of it? In England, a man was ordered by his landlord to take down the Halloween zombies he had erected in his yard because passing moms found them too "realistic."

Excuse me, ladies: You're saying they look too much like the *real* zombies you've met?

So that's the overweening parent side. Meanwhile, any and every company that can possibly exploit any worries about Halloween will. "I would like to introduce Bramble Berry's Halloween Bath Fizzies as a safe and fun Halloween activity," the product's publicist, Lindsey Greulich, wrote when I was asking around about new Halloween products.

The fizzies do look fun—you throw them into your bath, and they fizzle à la Alka Seltzer. But as a "safe" alternative to trick-or-treating? Or even as a "safe" new part of the holiday pantheon? Halloween has plenty of safe activities already, thank you very much: walking, begging, and gorging.

Speaking of which: "Take supplements!" the folks over at Culturelle have started suggesting at Halloween time. "Give your child a probiotic supplement, like Culturelle," they say. "Studies show it can greatly reduce the chance of getting allergic reactions and decrease the severity of red itchy skin associated with eczema (the number one symptom of food allergies)."

So now Halloween is a time for premedication, just like a liver transplant. (And imagine if kids finally *do* die from tainted candy. It will be *premedicated murder*.)

And then there are all the things you can buy to make sure that your children, should they actually venture out, eventually make it back home. Special lights to attach to their costumes. Glow-in-the-dark candy bags, ten bucks each. Cell phones they can use to call home throughout the night. (Not that they should be out at night. "Try to finish trick-or-treating before dark," Nationwide Hospital's safety tips suggest.)

And more advice, from all over. Don't share masks—they're germy. Come to think of it, don't wear masks—they restrict peripheral vision and can obstruct breathing. Don't wear a dark costume—hard to see. Or a loose costume—easy to trip on. Don't wear someone else's costume, comes a friendly reminder from the folks at Lice MD. Guess why.

Maybe kids shouldn't wear costumes at all.

Keep the phone number of poison control handy—that's another oft-offered piece of advice, even though we have just established that no one gets poisoned candy on Halloween. And do not use a knife to carve a pumpkin! The tip lists usually recommend using those little kits with the plastic saws you can buy at the grocery. Yet more crap for your home.

So now you've got a holiday where the costumes are too dangerous to wear, the candy too dangerous to eat, the pumpkins too dangerous to carve, and the neighborhood too dangerous to explore.

But you do have festive bathtub fizzies.

Happy Halloween.

REAL WORLD

Discuss with Neighbors What Treats Are Appropriate

Susan Purcell, the blogger behind Virtual Linguist, writes:

> Here in England, the Thames Valley Police have published a list of guidelines for Halloween on their "crime reduction" page:
>
> - Parents or a responsible adult should always accompany children to make sure that they stay safe.
> - Parents should identify neighbours who are willing to have trick or treat calls.
> - Make these neighbours aware of approximately what time you plan to call.
> - Discuss with these neighbours what treats are appropriate.
> - If money is given, identify a charity for this to be donated to.
> - Discuss what "tricks" are acceptable with your children.
> - Parents should discourage older children (teenagers) from trick or treating—it is an activity for young children. As a rule, if they are old enough to trick or treat on their own, they are too old to do it.
>
> You can also download a poster to display in your window, which says "No trick or treat: please enjoy your night without disturbing ours."

Going Free Range

Free-Range Baby Step: Let your kid wear a mask, borrow a costume, and carry a prop. Boo.

Free-Range Brave Step: Have your children, age nine and up, go trick-or-treating with friends you trust. Without you. Yes, *do* have them wear some reflective tape and only cross at corners. Cars are the danger on Halloween, not psychopaths.

Giant Leap for Free-Range Kind: Let them eat their candy without you examining it! Remember: Joel Best, the professor who made a *career* studying Halloween dangers, never examined his own kids' candy. (Except when he went to steal a KitKat.)

Study History

Your Ten-Year-Old Would Have Been Forging Horseshoes (or at Least Delivering Papers)

"**I** don't want my son to learn or think that that type of thing is OK."

That's what a parent wrote on Amazon regarding a DVD very clearly labeled "For adults."

Well of course! Why would anyone want a kid to watch adult videos? That's sick!

But . . . wait a sec. Her comment was about a DVD with Big Bird on its cover. And Bert. And Ernie. And Oscar and Grover and—what the heck is going on here?

The usual. Changing times.

The video in question is *Sesame Street: Old School, Vol. 1*. Released in 2006, it's a three-DVD highlight reel of the show's earliest years, 1969 to 1974. It's got classic clips like Oscar the Grouch singing "I Love Trash" and Ernie in the tub with his rubber ducky. That's not the stuff of adult videos, is it? (*Is it*? Please tell me no!)

The DVDs also show a whole lot of scenes of real, live children doing wild things like climbing on planks and playing in a vacant lot. They wiggle through a pipe. A couple of boys scramble to the top of a jungle gym (isn't that illegal now?), even as a preschooler pedals her trike, helmet-free. In a scene from the very first episode, a girl who's new to the neighborhood gets shown around by a stranger—male!—who takes her home for milk and cookies with his wife. All of which may have seemed nice and normal in 1969, but today looks like a trailer for *Saw VII: This Time It's Preschool.* In fact, maybe they could have saved everyone a lot of trouble if they just called the DVD *Nightmare on Sesame Street.*

"There were a lot of discussions about it," said a friend of mine who works at Sesame Workshop. Discussions, he admitted sheepishly, about whether they really had to slap a "For adults" warning on the DVD. The bigshots there must have known how ridiculous it would seem: putting a warning for kids on a show for kids. But their target market seems to have been the nostalgia crowd alone, so the warning says, "These early Sesame Street episodes are intended for adults and may not meet the needs of today's preschoolers."

As if today's preschoolers are genetically different from yesterday's preschoolers. (Us!) As if *Sesame Street* hadn't been vetted by a million educational specialists, even back then, who wanted to show only the most wholesome, safe, sunny-day vision of childhood that public television could possibly put together. So why is it adults-only viewing today?

Because our view of what children can do and figure out and survive is at its utter nadir. We can't imagine them not hurting themselves in a vacant lot, much less finding their way around the neighborhood without a trusted adult. (Not a stranger! Especially one promising cookies.) We don't want them to climb to the top of a jungle gym because we don't trust them to get back down without breaking something. Crawl through a pipe? That's for Indiana Jones. Our belief in our kids is so below-sea-level low that when the *New York Times* asked *Sesame Street*'s executive producer Carol-Lynn Parente (you cannot make these names up), Why doesn't the DVD include that classic skit where the Cookie Monster plays pipe-smoking Alistair Cookie—and ends up gobbling his pipe? Ms. Parente replied that this was because the skit "modeled the wrong behavior."

Like three-year-olds are really going to start smoking pipes? Or eating them? They're not! Pipes taste bad and are too big to cram into your mouth, and there's only about seven of them left in America anyway. To think of kids as that endangered is to forget a great truth:

Children are built to survive. And until very, very recently, adult survival depended on them, too.

That's because throughout most of human history, kids and adults worked side by side. There wasn't an age cutoff, like there is for kindergarten. All that mattered was competence, and because everyone could use an extra pair of hands, competence was greatly encouraged. As soon as young folks were able to, they fed animals, planted seeds, fetched water. They even managed to pick corn without turning the cobs into pipes they'd eat and choke to death on.

In other words, childhood was golden—to adults. Pampering was as far off as Pampers. Parents who could find their children apprenticeships with craftsmen were thrilled to pack them off for the next decade or so. Would they be treated well? Fed well? Given a blanket? There were no guarantees. But then again, the idea of treating children as cherished cherubs wasn't out there yet. Starvation was. Everyone, no matter how young, had to earn his keep. And, sometimes, his sheep.

"I used to be a slave. We were all slaves at one time or another." So said Abraham Lincoln, by which I think he meant that all young people were expected to do brutally hard work with very little say about it. And they were expected to start doing it at a very young age.

"In colonial America, especially in colonial New England, it was not uncommon to send off children who were very young— six, seven, eight, nine—to live with other families as servants," says Steven Mintz, a professor of history and author of *Huck's Raft: A History of American Childhood*. Six-year-olds might not have been in charge of something really dangerous, like cleaning out the chimney (although in England, it wasn't uncommon for kids to start that particular job at age four). But young colonists were certainly able to help cook and clean and run household errands. And if they weren't, an older person showed them how to do it so that they'd rise to the task in the future.

Now compare this idea—children expected to help out adults—with the *Lou and Lou Safety Patrol* mini-videos you can watch on the Playhouse Disney Web site.

Lou and Lou are cartoon characters whose voices are more annoying than any other characters in cartoon history, including Scrappy-Doo, Scooby's nephew (who makes Scooby sound like Winston Churchill). The Lous are a brother and sister of maybe three or four years old who call themselves the "Safety Patrol." They spring into action when their six- or sevenish sister actually wants to make their dad breakfast for his birthday.

"Not so fast!" squeak the safety-loving sibs as their sister tries to cook some eggs. "Never touch a pot or pan on the stove. Let a grown-up." They plunk an orange safety cone in front of the stove to keep her away.

Undaunted, the sister drifts down the counter and reaches for a knife. "You have a safety violation!" chime her bad cop–bad cop siblings. "You should always stay away from sharp knives and let a grown-up help if you need to slice something."

Now, I'm not saying that six-year-olds make the ideal short-order chefs and let's let 'em loose near the french-fry vat. But the constant refrain of "Get a grown-up! Let a grown-up!" reinforces the whole idea that, rather than trying to learn any kind of real-world skill, kids should sit back and leave it all up to the adults.

And by the way, what age are we talking about when we use that term? A survey by polling expert Tom Smith at the University of Chicago asked fourteen hundred people that very question: At what age do you think adulthood begins in the United States? The answer: twenty-six.

That's a long time to wait before you touch a sharp knife.

When parents (or children's TV producers) worry that kids can't possibly play safely on their own or make scrambled eggs or even, when they're in their tweens, ride their bikes to baseball, I always wonder what their own ancestors were doing at that age. Probably it was something a tad more demanding.

"Let's take Mark Twain for example," says Mintz. "Mark Twain's father dies when he's eleven or twelve and then he has to go to work and his childhood is over. He works as an apprentice printer in New York and Washington, D.C., and St. Louis and Keokuk, Iowa. So by the time he's eighteen he has lived by himself in New York and Washington." Not to mention the wild Midwest.

"Or let's take Herman Melville," the professor continues, enthused by the subject. "His father also dies when he's around twelve and temporarily he's put to work in a store. But eventually, around the age of sixteen, he's put on a whaling ship and goes out to the South Pacific. He abandons ship and he's captured by cannibals! So by the time he's eighteen or twenty, he's seen Hawaii." And almost been eaten.

Which is to say, maybe our own teenagers can manage to make their beds.

Last historic figure here: Ben Franklin. "At around twelve, he needed a career, so he and his father walked around Boston to see what jobs looked good," says Mintz. Some of the craftsmen charged a fee for their apprenticeships, "So it was cheaper to send him off to his much older brother." That brother, you may recall from American history class, was a printer who ran a newspaper where Ben began his writing career. When he absolutely couldn't get along with the brother anymore, Ben ran off to Philadelphia, dirt poor, but with something very valuable up his ruffled sleeve: a trade.

(And a key. But that's another story.)

Until the Industrial Revolution came along and turned children into cheap labor, children were the opposite: valuable labor. Either they helped out on the farm, as Honest Abe did, or they helped their masters, and in turn their masters taught them a skill by which they could eventually make a living. (Often after years and years of scut work.) Adults and children worked together, and there wasn't such a huge gulf between them. Not that children were considered mini-adults, unloved and exploited. Just that children were expected to rise to the adulthood all around them, not stew in adorable incompetence.

Fast-forward to our own generation, when we were kids. The generation that could watch uncensored *Sesame Street*. In just that short span of time between our own youth and our offsprings', two of the only jobs that had been left for kids have totally changed: paper delivery and baby-sitting.

It is now almost impossible to become a paperboy unless you are an adult. Calls to eight newspapers in North Carolina found exactly zero that would take anyone under age eighteen. Part of the reason is that the suburbs have spread out more, so they may require a car for the farthest reaches. And part of the reason is that hard-pressed adults became willing to take this job. But a big chunk is also that newspapers, eager to avoid any kind of legal hassles, now hire only licensed drivers with their own liability insurance. In other words, not a twelve-year-old with a Schwinn. So good-bye, for the most part, to paper routes and the idea that anyone under voting age could have that classic chance to demonstrate his—or her—fortitude, dependability, and throwing arm.

OK, so what about baby-sitters? That news, happily, is a little less dire. Plenty of kids, still mostly girls, continue to ply this ancient trade with refrigerator benefits. But they seem to start a little older, with generally less expected of them.

"I started baby-sitting at twelve, mostly babies and toddlers, some school-aged kids," says Sylke Finnegan, a mom in Portland, Oregon. Sometimes she baby-sat in the afternoon, but there were evening hours, too, sometimes past midnight.

Now she is a mother of a thirteen-year-old, but for her daughter—a year older than when Finnegan started baby-sitting—that job is not in the cards. "I will not leave her home alone for more than one hour. And never after dark."

Marti Lindsey, a forty-five-year-old mom in San Diego, wouldn't hire a thirteen-year-old anyway—even though she remembers when she started baby-sitting at age nine or ten. "I was very responsible for my age," says Lindsey. "Here's what blows me away today. When I was a kid, we had neighbors with small children, about ages two and three. When the husband was out of town, the wife needed to work—she was a nurse, working graveyard—I would stay overnight with the kids. I was like twelve or thirteen. But I would never dream of leaving my son, Max, with someone that young, even for a few hours."

These moms aren't outliers: they're right in step with today's society that assumes tweens are twits or, at least, irresponsible. What they forget is not only how responsible they were at that age but also that, until the recent advent of small families, it was often the older sisters who took care of the kids who came along. More about that in the next chapter.

Of course, by the time our ancestors were of baby-sitting age, the baby they were sitting was often their own—another fact grown conveniently foggy. I know that my great-grandma was married at age fifteen and had my grandmother shortly thereafter. She wasn't "fast." It wasn't a shotgun marriage. (Jews? Shotguns? Maybe someone lobbed a matzoh ball through the window.) That's just the age things were done back then. And if that seems unreasonable, imagine what our great-grandmothers would think if they saw our fifteen-year-olds hanging out at the mall with nothing to do but try on lip gloss and buy giant pretzels that always smell better than they taste.

Most of our great, great-grandparents—and theirs and theirs, all the way back—began having babies as soon as their hormones were up for it (so to speak), same as all other animals still do today. The deal was: reach puberty, create progeny. Obviously, our teenage ancestors must have been capable of raising children and keeping them safe and gathering enough food and passing along all their teenage wisdom, or we humans would have stopped dead in our tracks. We'd be dodo birds with opposable thumbs. The fact that our species is still here just proves how capable teens are: they got us to this point on the time line.

Of course, if adolescents are ready to take on the world—and make babies and sustain the species—it's no surprise they're surly and awful to be around when we treat them like little children today. The disconnect between "I'm grown up!" and "You're grounded" is just too great. One study found that the peak year for depression among American women is eighteen. They're ready to start out but can't get started. That's why, whether you want your child to become a printer's apprentice or smithy or tanner—or not—it would still be nice to have apprenticeships around.

Mintz found one for his son, "and it turned out to be the greatest experience," he says. "He was twelve and he worked as a computer techie at the university I was working at. So he was with all these 'bad influences'—guys who were in their early twenties—and he so admired them. He just thought these were the greatest guys on earth and it was really a good growing-up experience." At the time, the mini-Mintz hated school, but here was a chance for him to succeed someplace else: the "real world." Lucky kid! (And smart dad.)

Problem is, it's hard to find those experiences, even if you want your kid to work. It's even hard for under-eighteens to volunteer. Most organizations, just like those North Carolina newspapers, don't want to be bothered training youngsters or insuring them. That's why the closest our family has come to a work experience is for us to start—finally—requiring our kids to do some chores beyond picking up their socks. (Which itself requires near-constant prodding. And the occasional lobbed matzoh ball.)

Now when Izzy, eleven, has to do the dishes, he may complain, but he ends up feeling proud. Morry, our thirteen-year-old, complains too. They are both just fine complainers. ("Why me?" "Again?" "I did it *last* night!") But when we do get that older one dishwashing or—as we did one memorable afternoon—*vacuuming*, we hear him singing to himself. A burden, in a way, has lifted. He has something to do that makes a little difference in the world (and a huge difference to our carpet). He is just like those thousands of generations before him who got to skin deer.

We want our children to become fine, upstanding adults, but in some ways we treat them as long as possible as sweet, silly babies.

If it's impossible to have them help out on the farm or apprentice in a forge (no matter how cool that would look on college applications), the alternative is to have them help out in the family business of running the home. Or help out in someone else's home, by baby-sitting.

Have them smuggle in a DVD of *Sesame Street: Old School*, and you just might start a revolution.

REAL WORLD

The Old Man Beat Me Because I Didn't Like to Steal

In the early 1900s, the *New York Independent* gathered oral histories of ordinary folks. What was life like for young people back then? Here, edited, is the story of Rocco Corresca:

> When I was a very small boy, I lived in Italy in a large house with many other small boys who were all dressed alike and were taken care of by some nuns. It was a good place, on the side of the mountain, where grapes were growing and melons and oranges and plums.
>
> The nuns taught us our letters and how to pray, and we worked in the fields during the middle of the day. We always had enough to eat and sometimes there were feast days, when we marched about wearing flowers.
>
> Those were good times and they lasted till I was nearly eight. Then an old man came and said he was my grandfather. He showed some papers and cried over me and said he would take me to his beautiful home. But when we got there it was a dark cellar that he lived in and I did not like it at all. Very rich people were on the first floor. They had servants and plenty of good things to eat, but we were down below and had nothing. There were four other boys and the old

man said they were all my brothers. All were larger than I and they beat me till one day Francisco said that they should not, and then Paulo, who was the largest of all, fought him till Francisco drew a knife and gave him a cut. Then the old man knocked them both down with a stick and gave them beatings.

Each morning we boys all went out to beg, running to the carriages and getting in the way of the people so that they had to give us money or walk over us. The old man often watched us and at night he took all the money.

Begging was not bad in the summer because we went all over the streets and there was plenty to see, and if we got much money we could spend some buying things to eat. The old man knew we did that. He used to smell us to see if we had eaten anything, and he often beat us for eating when we had not eaten.

I was with the old man for three years. He beat me, too, because I didn't like to steal. Then one day he said to me: "If you don't want to be a thief you can be a cripple. That is an easy life and they make a great deal of money."

That night I heard him talking to one of the men that came to see him. He asked how much he would charge to make me a good cripple, like those that crawl. They had a dispute, but at last they agreed and the man said that I should be made so that people would shudder and give me plenty of money.

I was much frightened, but I did not make a sound and in the morning I went out to beg with Francisco. I said to him: "I am going to run away. I don't want to be a cripple, no matter how much money the people may give."

"Where will you go?" Francisco asked me.

"I don't know," I said, "somewhere."

He thought awhile and then he said, "I will go, too."

(continued on next page)

The boys ended up in a seaside village where a fisherman named Ciguciano took them in. He had them work on his boat, but treated them most decently. It sounds like Rocco fell in love with Ciguciano's daughter, Teresa. But five years later the boys—now sixteen and eighteen—left for America after a young man promised them untold riches.

Actually, he had sold them into the servitude of a rag dealer in Brooklyn. After a year of that, the boys escaped again, this time to a crew of sewer diggers in New Jersey. The Irish boss there taught them English. When there was no more digging to be done, they worked in a saloon where a bootblack showed them how to shine shoes. With the money they saved, the boys opened their own shoeshine parlor. And then another. Here's Rocco, finishing his story:

> I am 19 years of age now and have $700 saved. Francisco is 21 and has about $900. We shall open some more parlors soon.
>
> Francisco and I have a room to ourselves now and some people call us "swells." Ciguciano always said that we should be great men. Francisco bought a gold watch with a gold chain as thick as his thumb. He is a very handsome fellow and I think he likes a young lady that he met at a picnic.
>
> I often think of Ciguciano and Teresa. He is a good man, one in a thousand, and she was very beautiful. Maybe I shall write to them about coming to this country.

Going Free Range

Free-Range Baby Step: Watch
Sesame Street: Old School with
your *Sesame Street*–age child. Try not to weep for days gone by.

Free-Range Brave Step: Help your child, age nine or up, find an "apprenticeship." If you can find a neighborhood business or volunteer organization willing to give your child some regular responsibility, fantastic. But because this has been hard to do for the last century or so, you might have to try an apprenticeship inside the home. Starting as young as age two, kids can help sort the laundry into "colors" and "whites." (It may be the last time they find this fascinating.) By four they can help clear the table. Come age five or six they can sweep (but not totally into the dustpan), and by second grade they can start making their own lunches and taking out the garbage. Third grade or so? They can do the dishes. Maybe you're already on the ball with this, but we didn't start serious (or even simple) chore-requiring until just this year—grades 5 and 7. Secretly, we've been shocked at how meekly our sons assumed the yoke. If we'd known that being taskmasters was going to be this easy, we'd have started about half a decade earlier. (Oh, and did I mention we pay them a dollar a day, just to do things they really should be doing anyway, including make their beds? Still—we're glad they have "jobs" now, and so are they.)

One Giant Leap for Free-Range Kind: When you find yourself thinking, "Gee, I'd like my son to get to choir practice by himself, but what if he gets lost?" or "My daughter thinks she's ready to baby-sit, but what if there's an emergency?" remember Rocco's story—how much he went through, how young. It will give you a surprising jolt of courage.

Be Worldly

Why Other Countries Are Laughing at zee Scaredy-Cat Americans

Would you hire a nanny who is five years old?

Perhaps not. Yet around the world (not to mention throughout history), study after Ph.D.-garnering study has found that 40 to 80 percent of all toddlers are cared for by their older siblings. Siblings who may just be a year or two older than the kids they're bringing up.

It works like this. One day the baby is king of the roost, suckling at the breast, and the next day—wham. Mom has to go back to work picking coffee or pounding maize, or maybe she's about to give birth again, so dealing with the baby is more than she can handle. She rubs hot pepper balm on her nipples—really, that's the way they do it in some parts of the world—and a very startled baby suddenly realizes, Whoa! The good ol' days are gone forever. Now he's a toddler, and toddle he must—away from Mom, off to his new life with the other kids.

Indeed, says David Lancy, a professor at Utah State University and author of *The Anthropology of Childhood*, in more than one culture, "a mother is chastised if she is overly fond of her child." Her job is to reject the child so that the child has no choice but to join the group of youngsters who take care of each other and keep themselves occupied so their parents can work. Think of it as on-site day care, without the baby wipe warmers.

"The adored small child must suffer the trauma of growing into an object of contempt," is how Lancy rather baldy describes it. And although that's probably not a technique you're going to find front and center in most parenting magazines—"Top Tips for Banishing Baby," "Hot Pepper Balms Your Breasts Will Love," "Ready, Set, Reject!"—it just happens to work really well in about half the world.

The older siblings, usually girls, teach their young wards the basics: how to eat, go to the bathroom, start fetching things. In fact, they don't really teach. They don't have to. It's not diagramming sentences. The toddlers mostly learn by observing. And by the time they're two, maybe two and a half, they're full-fledged playmates. In the Liberian village where Lancy lived for a while with a tribal chieftain and his four wives (the tribal chieftain's four wives, that is; Lancy was single at the time), Lancy had a hard time figuring out which child belonged to which mother, because the children mixed and mingled so much. Also because they had so little to do with their moms. (The dad barely knew their names.)

Outside, the village children would all end up at the "Mother Ground," a living-room-size lot that was the unofficial park, where they'd play all day. Although there'd usually be some older person nearby—a granny spinning, for instance—"days would go by without any adult intervention," Lancy said.

The kids were all right. "On average," he observed, "village children seem more consistently ebullient than their privileged suburban counterparts."

You knew that was coming, of course. The kids who figure out how to play with each other always do seem happiest. And then there's that other inevitable irony: material wealth cannot win versus actual, kids-running-around fun.

When my son Izzy and I were watching that *Sesame Street: Old School* video the other day (to review it for this very book), there was a scene of about eight kids playing follow the leader. They climbed on a picnic table and skipped through construction material.

"Did you ever play that?" I asked.

His head shook, and my heart sank. It's only about the oldest game in the world, and he'd never even been exposed to it—the freewheeling fun of following a goofy leader or, better still, the joy of being a small but potent dictator: follow ME! All of you! Now! Onto the fence!

Then again, my children have never been exposed to the joy of beriberi, either, or the joy of hunger or oozing sores or dragging brackish water from a faraway well and subsisting on cornmeal mush with little stones in it. So maybe I'll stop romanticizing childhood in impoverished villages (and *Sesame Street*) and get to the point:

What we think of as normal child rearing is not the way a lot of other countries do it. And activities we consider far "too risky" for our kids do not make the smallest blip on other countries' risk radar screens. Even the ones rich enough to *have* radar screens. Let us go to some of those more affluent spots on the globe to see how they, too, differ from us. In fact, let's start with a really affluent one: Sweden, land of the midnight sun. And gummy fish.

Rita Sunden's husband is CEO of a company that makes the blades for the windmills that make electricity. Naturally, this is something those clean-living, bike-riding Swedes would like, so a while back, Rita's family moved there. The Sundens have four children, and when their oldest daughter was thirteen, in eighth grade, her class went on a field trip from their town of thirty-five thousand down to Stockholm, the country's biggest city. After a morning of supervised sightseeing, "the teacher said, 'Okay. Come back in three hours,'" recalls Sunden. And that was the remainder of the field trip: we've taken you around for a few hours, now go take yourselves. Have fun. Explore. And get back on time. Which is what everyone did.

A few years later, the Sundens were back in the United States, living in Lake Forest, Illinois. Lake Forest is where they set the movie *Ordinary People*. (A movie, my friend once memorably noted, that was not called *Ordinary Incomes*.) The place is beyond upscale suburban lovely. It's mansion filled. It's hushed. It's where Jennifer Aniston and what's-his-name were looking for a house, when they were a couple. (Then they costarred in *The Break-Up*, and did.).

By this time, another of Rita's daughters had reached eighth grade, and she too went on a field trip—to the local park. "They were playing games and team-building outside, and it was on the street we lived on, about half a mile away," says Rita. Rita herself was an hour away, having lunch with friends. Then her cell phone rang.

It was the school calling to say that her daughter had had a nose bleed and needed to go home to change her clothes. "I said, 'Well, just send her home. She's got a key. She can change and come right back.' They said, 'Nope. Can't be done. Someone has to come get her.'" Rita ended up calling a neighbor who came by to pick the girl up, escort her home, and then escort her safely back to her teacher.

Two different countries. Two different ideas of what a thirteen-year-old can do.

If we can't understand the freewheeling folks in other countries who let their kids out of their clutches, they sure cannot understand us. "I am living in Germany and from here it looks like big, strong America has vanished," wrote Thomas Prosi, a dad of two tweens. "When we were young, we looked up to America. We liked that freedom, the opportunities and the rights people seemed to have over there. But now? The land of the free? The home of the brave?"

Insert Germanic guffaw here. (Then insert, from me, a little dig about how maybe we're overprotective, but at least we don't start world wars.) Anyway, how is modern-day childhood in Germany different from childhood in the United States?

Christine Hohlbaum is a Boston writer transplanted to small-town Germany with her German-born husband. They have a boy, seven, and girl, nine, and they were recently visited by Christine's sister, who still lives in Boston and has children almost the exact same age.

"My daughter and son met up with some friends to go to the tree for chestnuts," says Christine, talking about the local tree the way we talk about the local Starbucks. "It's probably a five-minute walk from my house, but my sister could not *believe* that I felt comfortable enough to have my kids actually go out by themselves."

But off Christine's kids went, free as squirrels (and with the same objective), because walking and nature time are both given top priority in Germany. Fresh air rules. Driving the kids everywhere? *Nein*.

Car culture contributes to a lot of the differences between America and the rest of the world, especially when it comes to how kids spend their time. Americans are in their cars more than most everyone else because we've got a huge country, and we just keep filling it up (not unlike our backseats). As the suburbs continue to expand, so does the amount of time kids spend in the car, and it just keeps getting worse.

One of the reasons for this is that maxed-out homeowners haven't wanted to spring for sidewalks. So in newish town after newish town, it is almost impossible—or at least, extremely scary—to walk or ride a bike where you or your kids might want to go. The result? Even more car rides: to the store, to karate, to that increasingly common destination, the school bus stop. (Parents don't want their kids walking *anywhere*.)

This car cocooning struck not only Anne Bell upon her return from a stint in Dusseldorf, Germany, but also her four-year-old daughter, who was already used to walking freely.

"One day," says Anne, a news show publicist, "she literally sat down in front of me and she looked over her shoulder like a driver and said, 'I'm the mommy and you're the little girl and you're *bored* because you're just waiting to get somewhere.'" This was her way of protesting the chauffeured life she'd suddenly been buckled into. "It's such a nice day, Mommy. Can't we walk to school?" she asked— over and over. But the answer was always no. Her family lives on a busy Virginia street with no shoulder, much less a sidewalk. Ride she must.

In the rest of the world, most children do walk to school, and they start at age five or six or seven. Their parents do not accompany them. By age ten or sometimes even before that, kids may board a public bus to get to school, and no one looks at them askance. The other riders know that children are capable of getting around, and they don't consider this a rogue activity.

"Kids are expected to exert independence very early, initially in minor ways," says Abi Sutherland, a San Francisco software designer now living with her family in a small town in The Netherlands. "Many stores have a *kinderhoek*—a kid's corner—where children can play while their parents shop. Adults are frequently out of sight of their kids for long periods of time." And that's not only true at the store. Abi's four-year-old is allowed to go to the playground down her street, unaccompanied, if she tells Abi where she's going first. Who's there? Other friends. Says Abi, "There are almost never any parents at the playground accompanying their kids."

That's the kind of freedom Anne Bell's preschooler was pining for.

Unsupervised playgrounds seem to be the norm in most countries, freeing up parents to do other things if they choose. Another parenting perk in some parts is unofficial child care. Mothers in Mexico, Hungary, and Vietnam all told me about their delightful experiences with kids and the kitchen help in local restaurants.

In Hanoi, says Megan Deveaux, a Canadian who had spent the previous year in Vietnam with the United Nations, part of restaurant workers' pay often comes in the form of housing—usually right above the restaurant. This works out nicely for any parents well off enough to dine below, because if their kids get bored or start to cry, "They take them upstairs," says Megan. "They" being the kitchen help. "Upstairs" being their apartment.

"They play games or let them look at the kitchen or look at their bedroom. They see it as a service they're providing while the parents eat," Megan says. Because service is unhurried anyway, and there's usually more staff than necessary, parents linger as different waiters play with the children. The basic assumption on the part of the diners is that their kids are safe. The child care is great. Let's have another glass of wine.

Parents in other countries just seem to trust their children and their fellow citizens more. Or at least, parents in non-English-speaking countries seem to. Parents in Britain and Canada and Australia all seem to be just about as worried as Americans about stranger danger and abduction. The English even insist that anyone who is going to work in any capacity with children—be it as a scout leader, school volunteer, or cupcake-baking class mom—undergo a police check first. No official OK, no contact with kids. The underlying assumption appears to be that because you are suspiciously interested in young people, you'd better prove you are not a convicted pedophile.

So it's not like the entire world is more happy-go-lucky than Americans when it comes to kids. But most of it is. What happens if you're torn between both outlooks, unsure of what really makes sense? Sophi Gilliland, a missionary living in Eastern Europe, is dealing with that right now . . . and starting to lean toward one side.

"I am a mom of four. I have two blue-eyed, light-haired girls ages four and five, and two dark-featured boys ages nine and thirteen," she wrote to Free-Range Kids. "Until recently, we lived in Los Angeles. While we were there, the probation officer who lived across the street made a comment to me that I should watch my kids closely because I had a 'pedophile smorgasbord.'"

That one remark turned Sophi into a nervous wreck. She didn't want to let her children play outside anymore, even with each other, without her standing right there. *Smorgasbord. Smorgasbord.* She kept envisioning the worst (and Swedish meatballs). And then she moved to Lithuania. I gave her a call. "They leave their baby carriages, with the baby inside, outside the stores where they shop," Sophi reports from her new home. Children walk to school along the busy freeway. On school vacations, when both parents have to work, the kids stay home, alone. They cook for themselves and play. They ride their bikes over to their friends' homes. All of which had Sophi reeling.

"When I was here the first year, I read a book—every chapter was on a different child abduction and how that child was able to escape. It was basically how to childproof your kid from being abducted, and my friends here were saying, 'Stop reading that! You're freaking yourself out!'"

But when she lived in California, Sophi continued, "We watched so much TV, and the news is always talking about this child being snatched, and that one, and this kid went into the bathroom and some guy killed him, that you become very scared someone is on the prowl for your children. And you think you are being instinctively protective. But then you come to Lithuania and nobody's being like that, and you realize: what I thought was 'instinct' was sheer cultural fear."

Now, Sophi says, she is still afraid for her children's safety, but . . . less so. She's feeling a little more Lithuanian. For instance, normally she picks her kids up from school. But recently she let her nine-year-old son, Ezra, take the bus with his friend to that friend's home for the weekend. She gave her son her cell phone "just in case," but he didn't use it. He just had fun with his buddy, and the families reunited in church on Sunday morning. "A whole weekend out of my sight in a foreign country!" says Sophi. "It's hard to let go, isn't it?" But she did.

As Sophi tries to sort it all out—what's sane, what's safe, how much supervision makes sense—she's doing what I hope this chapter does: throwing some cultural assumptions into the air. You may recall a time all of America was asked to do that, about ten years ago.

It happened when a Danish woman on vacation in New York did as the Danes (and, apparently, Lithuanians) do: she parked her sleeping daughter in her stroller outside a restaurant and then went in to have dinner with the baby's father, a New Yorker. Next thing you know, the parents were under arrest for child endangerment.

Endangerment? The mom thought she was giving her baby exactly what all babies need: nice spring air!

The incident became raging tabloid fodder for a week—sane mom? crazy mom?—as the baby was whisked off to foster care and the parents were whisked off to prison. Three days later they were released on the following condition: don't do this again within six months, and we won't press charges. The Danish mom didn't stick around to test the system. She rushed back to Denmark, daughter in tow.

The Danish newspapers were outraged. After all, leaving kids outside unattended is common practice there, a sign of good sense, not neglect. But as New York's commissioner of child services remarked, it was not up to America "to make inquiries about whether this is acceptable in Denmark."

But maybe it is. Maybe by looking at the way other countries treat their children—the freedom they are given, the responsibilities those kids assume, the way adults trust each other—we can figure out which parts of our parenting culture really make sense, and which parts are just strange cultural quirks, like eating marshmallow bits in our cereal or getting a bikini wax on the way to Tibetan meditation class.

Or, come to think of it, reading books about child rearing that say, "Don't read books about child rearing."

REAL WORLD

After a Week of Spying, I Finally Relaxed

Angelina Hart, a Free-Range Mom, writes:

> When I was living in Japan, everyone on the street let their kids go to the park alone. My daughters were 3 and 5 and just ran off with the other kids. I followed, ducking behind cars so they couldn't see me, and watched from a distance. They were all fine. After a week of spying I finally relaxed enough to enjoy the time that they were at the park.
>
> My brother grew up in Germany in the '60s and three years old was the official age when a child was old enough to go to the corner bakery in the morning to pick up the bread. Today, three years old is still thought of as infancy! Many people still have a 3-year-old in a high chair!
>
> One other story: A family I know traveled to Southeast Asia with their 2-year-old still in a stroller. All the local people thought the child had stumbled across a landmine. When the child got up and walked around they were amazed, but confused: Why would a healthy child need a wheelchair? Good question!

Going Free Range

Free-Range Baby Step: Ask a friend of yours who is from another country to tell you what he or she finds odd (or deranged) about child rearing here.

Free-Range Brave Step: Give yourself an International Day. Have your first-grade (or older) child walk to school, as she would in most of the rest of the world. Or, at the grocery store with your grade-school children, have them go get you things from other aisles. Just let them know where you'll be so you don't keep missing each other. They will feel proud and independent and, as the mom living in the Netherlands pointed out, so will you. This isn't quite as dramatic as dropping them off in a kiddie corner the whole time, as she does, but it's a start.

Meanwhile, if your children are in their teens, visit another city and let them explore on their own for a couple of hours. Give them a map, some cash, and a time and place to meet. (But don't be an idiot: make sure they write down that info.)

Giant Leap for Free-Range Kind: If you can afford it, travel outside the country with your children and try going native a little. If the local kids go marketing, let yours. If the kitchen help are willing to entertain your children, let them. Or go to restaurant in Denmark or Lithuania and park your child outside next to someone else's. Have a lovely meal!

Commandment 10

Get Braver

Quit Trying to Control Everything. It Doesn't Work Anyway

You remember the Steven Wright joke: "You can't have every-thing. Where would you put it?"

Same thing goes for control. You can't have total control. What would you do with it?

Say that somehow, one day, you meet the Parenting Genie (no relation to the Diaper Genie), and for a few wild weeks, she grants you TC—Total Control. Control of your kids, their school, their time. Maybe even how they answer the phone.

So you use your TC to make sure your scrawny son gets a place on the football team. Works like a charm! (Because it *is* a charm.)

The big game comes, he gets tackled by a 220-pounder, and—SNAP—he breaks his leg. By golly, your TC *didn't* work! So you press TC Rewind, and this time you make your son absent the day of the big game, so he doesn't get tackled. Your TC is working!

But without a broken leg, your son never ends up in the emer-gency room, where he would have fallen in love with medicine and healing and decided right then and there to become a doctor at the Albert Schweitzer Clinic in Gabon. Or at least a lobbyist for big pharma.

So you use TC to *let* him break that leg and find his true calling, but by the time he gets back to school he has missed his English class when they were teaching the word *hirsute,* so he screws up on his SATs, thereby missing the cutoff for his college by one point and so the TC worked . . . and didn't work . . . and it worked and it didn't and . . . it's complicated, isn't it?

Luckily for us there's no such thing as Total Control, since it would drive us absolutely crazy.

Unluckily for us, we act as if there were.

There is an idea in the air that somehow, if we just involve ourselves enough in our children's lives and think ahead and make a lot of plans and decisions, our children will be able to sail through their days, happy and successful.

As we shall see from the rest of this chapter, which involves sage advice from a lot of smart, psychologically minded professionals, this idea is, to use the technical term, "nuts."

I know I said don't trust experts, but these folks I do trust, because they're not "parenting" experts. They're *parent* experts. People who understand and empathize with us. Helpful folks. Especially when it comes to the big kahuna of parenting. Yes. Control.

Control is a figment of our imagination. Seeking it only makes us more anxious. It certainly isn't required for good child rearing. And to the extent that we *do* manage to solve all our children's problems—or keep those problems from ever even popping up—we are doing them a disservice. Not a fatal one that will stunt our children forever. But still, we are steering them away from the real source of confidence and independence, which comes from navigating the world and its surprises. Especially the unpleasant ones.

Since it is hard to suddenly give up an illusion as cherished as control, this chapter will discuss not only how to start letting go of it but also how to feel less awful as you do. And it'll discuss letting go of worry, too, since that's just another form of control. (You know how you bend sideways when you're worried that your bowling ball is about to fall into the gutter, and you think you can will it back on track by leaning and twisting? That's worry-as-control. Futile, but natural.) As you'll see, what helps the most in all of this is helping our kids prepare for the big, wide world.

Finally, at the end of this whole psychological journey, you and I will join each other for a beer or latte or giant brownie—if only metaphorically—because we have been dumped into these weird parental times, and it's hard getting sane, and we deserve a gosh-darn break. The kids can go watch TV.

For starters, are we really more worried than our parents? Haven't parents always worried?

Of course they have, says historian Peter Stearns, author of *Anxious Parents*. But what we've seen in just the last fifteen or twenty years is a leap off the charts. "Extravagant worry" is what he calls it. Extravagant in that it inflates remote possibilities into looming threats that we think we have to watch out for. Whether we're fearing for our children's physical safety or their psychological well-being ("How dare that teacher give his dinosaur diorama a D?!"), our job as parents has become much more demanding. We have to be on our toes all the time.

If we really think that a child could be abducted at any minute, for instance, we can't just let our kids walk to school the way we did. We have to drive them there or wait at the bus stop with them, both of which take up a lot of time, even while ratcheting up the very anxiety they're supposed to allay. *Why* are we at the bus stop that kids used to wait at alone? Because now it's way too scary. Why is it too scary? Because if it weren't scary, why would we all be waiting there? We're all at the bus stop because we're all at the bus stop. Worry is contagious.

As it escalates, so does the definition of "good parent." Chances are, your parents didn't attend absolutely every soccer practice or gymnastics lesson, but now a lot of us do. Sometimes it's fun—we get to watch the kids frolic, and also to gossip with the other parents. But sometimes we'd rather be doing something else. Anything else. Cleaning the oven. Flossing. Pulling hair wads out of the drain. Yet there we are, freezing (or baking) in the bleachers. Our job is to be ever present: encouraging, witnessing, and, often enough, electronically documenting. Then, depending on personal parenting style, we either make a keepsake scrapbook with an adorable felt cover or forget to download the photos for a year. But still, we were there. And any time we can't be? At the very least we can always go back to Parental Plan A: worrying.

My best friend from Chicago has confessed that whenever she and her twelve-year-old daughter are shopping at the mall but go to separate ends of the food court to get lunch, "I'm nervous the whole time till she comes back." That's usually about five minutes.

"Why?" I've asked. "Your daughter is as tall as I am. She's smart. She's in a public place. She's not going to go off with some guy offering her free candy." (Free Abercrombie shirts? Hmmm.)

"I know," said my friend. "But I just feel comfortable worrying."

How can worrying feel good?

"The idea is that if you're worrying, then you're doing the right thing," says Lawrence Balter, a professor at New York University and editor of the encyclopedia *Parenthood in America*. Worrying "is like a demonstration to yourself that you're being responsible," he says. It has become our national pastime.

Then there are the other, more active ways we are expected to protect and direct our children. One of the ways most of us do this from the second we wake up to the second we go to bed is: we keep our cell phones on.

As discussed a bit earlier, I am a big fan of cell phones, yet ambivalent about them too. My boys are out with one right now, so they can call and tell me where they're going after they finish up helping out at the school's bake sale. (Why is Mom not helping out at the bake sale, you ask? She is writing this Free-Range book, trying to take her own advice and let them have a little adventure on their own. Albeit an adventure in a familiar place, supervised by a lot of other moms, and probably involving the vast ingestion of cupcakes.)

Where were we? Oh yes. On the phone. The point is this: when people wonder, *How did parenting become so much more child-intensive so fast?* one of the answers is, "Simple. We signed up for that friends and family calling plan."

The cell phone means we are always connected to (and attempting to control) our kids.

"In the middle of a session," reports New Jersey psychiatrist Steve Resnick, "people will answer their phone. Sometimes they'll say, 'Honey, I'm in the doctor's office, I'll call you back in 50 minutes.' But some will say, 'I'm going to be home around six, I'll pick up some milk and do you want me to get pizza?'"

Most of these calls are from their kids, says Resnick. And far from feeling embarrassed that they have interrupted what was supposed to be the one part of the week devoted to their own mental health, most of the phone answerers feel they did the right thing. They were "there" for their kids.

Contrast this with Resnick's own lower-tech parents and childhood: "If my parents wanted to find me they'd have to call around to three or four houses and say, 'Is Steve over there? I need to remind him of this or that,'" recalls Resnick. "It was a hassle for them to do and it was an imposition on the other families, and there was a good chance I was outside anyway. So it forced them to be more hands-off and trust my choices."

That struck Resnick as so psychologically sound that these days he often forgoes his own cell phone and only uses a beeper. With a beeper, someone has to call him, leave a phone number, and wait for him to call back when it's convenient.

"I don't want it to be that easy to get ahold of me," says the shrink. "I want people to be aware that it's a little hassle for them and for me. If it's important enough, they'll do it. But if it's a little thing, it makes them not call me." That's true even for his daughters, ages twelve and fourteen.

I still remember the time my older son, Morry, who was maybe ten at the time, called me just after I'd left for work to ask if he could have banana bread for breakfast. "Sure!" I said. But what I should have said was, "Heck yes! Have whatever you want! *I'm not there*. If I get home and find the dregs of a vodka smoothie in the blender, I'll know you need more supervision. Otherwise, you know how to make breakfast, and you're old enough to decide what to eat."

The cell phone keeps the parent-child relationship back where it was when the kids were very young and needed constant supervision. When parents are always available to tell their kid what to do, they will, even when otherwise the kid would start making decisions himself. And wailing on the banana bread.

The assumption behind constant availability is that there are problems facing your child that must be solved, immediately, by you. The assumption behind *that* assumption is that you, the parent, are capable of solving all problems. And the secret assumption behind the assumption behind the . . . whatever, is that your child is helpless without you. So if you don't solve each and every problem, he's sunk, and you haven't done your job.

In other words, we are back to the issue of control.

The belief in control is the belief that if we do the right thing or make the right decision, everything will turn out fine. And if we don't, there will be hell to pay.

In real life, it's that feeling we get when we see the shortest line at the grocery and stand in it and breeze through. We took control! It's also responsible for the apoplexy we feel when we choose the shortest line and the lady in front of us turns out to be returning a tin of anchovies and she doesn't have the receipt and the cashier has to call the supervisor, who saunters over while chatting with her friend and then no one can find the cash register key and if only you'd gotten in the line to your right, you'd be halfway home by now and life does not seem one iota fair. We planned . . . the grocery laughed.

The more nice things we have in this world, the more we believe in control. So if we have a decent job, we believe that we made it happen. If we have a decent house, same thing. If our kids are doing fine, we assume that's under our control too. In fact, when things are pretty much humming, it looks as if we can control everyone else's lives as surely as we control everyone else's windows from the driver's seat.

But that's where we're wrong. We are not really, actually, always in the driver's seat. Or at least there's a driving instructor next to us with his own set of brakes, and his name is Luck or Fate or God or Bobo. (But probably Luck or Fate or God.) And the reason we even believe we're the ones in control is that we're in a very nice car called the First World.

It's an SUV.

The First World has air bags—literally and figuratively—and it has eradicated so many of the horrors that used to harm children, from lead in dinner plates to concrete under jungle gyms, that we don't think anything awful is supposed to happen to children anymore, at least not to children whose parents are taking care.

"Since the nineteenth century," says historian Stearns, "we've progressively come to believe that if something bad happens to a kid, parents have to have done something wrong. That's a huge trip. And ironically, it got worse when children *stopped* dying. When it became so rare for children to die, it became absolutely unacceptable for them to die. And even though it was unlikely, now you had to worry: Maybe they will."

Got that? The more safe our children became, the more we started to worry about them, because now if anything dangerous *did* happen to them, it would clearly be our fault. Fate has gone out the (electric) window, replaced by parental omnipotence. And it is this belief in control combined with the fear of screwing up that is driving us mad.

"Trying to control everything is impossible," says Allison Cohen, a psychotherapist in California. "It's like a hamster on a wheel, running, running, running. You're trying to know what's going to happen next and manage it perfectly." Yet you can't. Life is not chess, something where you can plan seventeen moves ahead, and even if it were, chess is really hard and requires utter concentration. Think of those weirdos who become chess champions. Now try thinking like them:

Your daughter is going to cheerleading practice after school, and she's usually hungry after that, so you should probably have a snack ready for her, agreed? But if she eats at five, she may not be hungry for dinner. That means she'll be hungry right before bed, so bedtime gets delayed by a late-evening bite, which means she'll be tired the next day, and tomorrow's a math test so . . . no snack after cheerleading practice? Or say you *do* give her a snack and she blows her math test—was it your fault because of everything you did or didn't do that led up to it?

That may sound like a convoluted example, but I know I find myself thinking that way sometimes (and driving my husband up the wall, especially when it has to do with pickup arrangements). In any event, it's just part and parcel of what we've been led to believe: that if we're smart enough and on the ball, we can smooth the way for our kids. This isn't just helicoptering—watching from above. In some countries (the colder ones), it's the phenomenon of the curling parent. So-called because in the game of curling, players frantically sweep the ice in front of a stone as it glides on its way. God forbid it should hit a bump or a scratch or a snowflake and go any direction but straight toward its goal.

The problem with trying to parent that way is as simple as it is ironic: "Attempting to control everything actually increases anxiety," says psychotherapist Cohen.

So now we're back to worry.

Think of a person with Obsessive Compulsive Disorder, says Harvey Roy Greenberg, a Manhattan psychiatrist. That person gets up in the morning and has to arrange the pillows on his bed *just so* or, he worries, something terrible will happen. He has to avoid touching the doorknob or something terrible will happen. He has to eat his Grape Nuts out of the Flintstones bowl or something terrible will happen. He has all these little things he believes he has to do or—poof—the world will fall apart.

"All of this is driven by a kind of insane feeling of omnipotence," says Greenberg. It's a belief "that you can exert all power over all things." And when it comes to your children, "you think you can lay down a magic carpet and conjure up spells that will guarantee your child absolute security. Good luck to that!"

This desire to control our children's lives is so similar to obsessive compulsion, which in itself is so similar to phobias (fearing for our kids, fearing our power to ruin the world, fearing . . . everything else) that Greenberg actually recommends that anxious parents try some of the calming exercises he uses on his patients.

"For instance, when we're treating somebody for a dog phobia," says Greenberg, "we ask them to visualize the dog from a mile away. Then half a mile away. Then across the street." The whole idea is to confront a fear steadily but gradually, until the person becomes "desensitized" to it.

In terms of parenting, the way to gradually desensitize ourselves to the fear of letting our kids go is to—you guessed it—gradually start letting them go. With input from us, natch, and oversight too. So for a week you walk your child to school, reminding her to take note of the streets and always to look both ways. When you see her doing that successfully, you walk her halfway, if that's what feels right. When even that starts to feel unnecessary, you let her walk the whole route, with a friend or solo. Peter Stearns, the *Anxious Parents* author, recommends letting kids walk to school without you starting in first grade. And he has eight children.

"I told one parent, 'Dig your fingernails in if you have to!'" says life coach Rebecca Kiki Weingarten, remembering a client who was afraid to let her son go on his first sleepover. But after the client talked it over with Weingarten and with the other boy's mom, the time came. "She showed me the marks in her palm," says Weingarten. Deep. But she sent her boy off.

Worrying is not an unreasonable thing for parents to do, adds Resnick, the psychiatrist. After all, something *could* happen. The problem is the out-of-proportion worry. If you can just put the risk in perspective, the fear gets put in perspective too. To do that, many shrinks suggest making an actual, pen-and-paper list of twenty things that could possibly go wrong during the activity you're worried about and then coldly contemplating the list. Which things are really likely? What can you do to prepare your child for them?

Remember the mom in Commandment 1 who was terrified to hear that her ten-year-old was at an ice cream parlor with a lot of friends and parents, but no adult directly chaperoning her? Resnick would counsel her to think of specific bad things that could happen to the girl: Is she going to overeat? Is she going to run out of the restaurant and get hit by a truck? Is she going to talk to some sleazy guy who comes over and tries to pick her up?

Nothing worse than a tummyache will transpire from overeating, and the mom knows the girl won't up and run out into the street, so those worries are off the list. But what if, strangely enough, some guy actually does harass her daughter?

"Say he's a gross guy," Resnick proposes. "So she comes home and says, 'Mom, this, like, really weird guy came over, and he said dirty words.' You give her a hug and let her have an extra scoop of ice cream, and it's not that bad."

So now, instead of just dreading "something terrible," the fear is very specific and, as it turns out, not that scary after all.

OK, OK—what if that mom's deepest, darkest, most unshakable fear was *really* that the gross guy would convince her daughter to come out to his suspiciously windowless van, and that was—the end? That's when the mom has to do three things. One: believe in her daughter's good judgment. Two: believe in the odds. (Statistically, her child is forty times more likely to die in the car ride home from Friendly's than at the hands of a murderous stranger.) And three: believe in herself. As a mom, she has undoubtedly given her girl some lessons about life and safety. She must believe she has had some effect.

An exercise like this reminds us that we always have a chance to prepare our children for the outside world. If we say to them, all along, "Don't go off with strangers" (a much more helpful lesson than "Don't talk to strangers"), they'll know not to. Remind them that you'll love them no matter what, and they won't feel embarrassed to tell you about the sleazy guy. And please do teach them not to run out into the street.

One mom I heard of told a friend that she didn't feel she had to teach her daughter any of this stuff because "I'll always be with her, so she doesn't need it."

In other words, Mom thinks she'll always be in control.

Right.

Really what this means is that any time she's *not* with her daughter, she will worry, because she has done nothing to help her child fend for herself. Her child will worry, too. That's not fair. Walk a kid to school, she has transportation for a day. Teach a kid to walk to school and she has transportation for a lifetime. (But with any luck she'll graduate by age eighteen.)

It should be obvious that our goal is to raise young people who can eventually get along without us, but clearly, we are living in weird, warped parenting times. Work on banishing the fantasy of always being in control, and, ironically, you'll feel less worried. But first, let's go have that drink. And the latte. And the giant brownie.

REAL WORLD

I Know a 6-Year-Old Who Still Rides in a Buggy

From Dr. Jo, a Free-Range pediatrician in England who tries to help parents get a grip on their worries:

> There's a preschool just down the road in my small country village with a stone wall round it. None of the children can get over it, and there have never been any accidents, but lots of people are clamoring to have a 6-feet-high fence round it so that the boogey man can't snatch their children.
>
> We lived in an even smaller village with a garden at the front of my home when I was growing up. One woman wanted to buy our cottage, but her sister advised her not to in case someone snatched her daughter from the garden.
>
> A 7-year-old had the best party ever in July—a camping party. The girl lives on a farm in the midst of fields, but one child was not allowed to go unless her mother came too . . . and shared a 2-man tent with her, rather than allowing her to share it with her friends.

(continued on next page)

And I know a mother whose 6-year-old daughter rides in a double buggy with the 4-year-old. They're under what looks like a giant see-through tent, just in case the darlings get a drip on them in the rain. This mother also covered up all the oak flooring in their barn conversion in case one of the children slipped. She has large pieces of foam under all the coffee tables in case one of the children, when they were younger, went underneath, sat up, and bumped their heads.

See? We are just as neurotic as you Americans!

Going Free Range

Free-Range Baby Step: Warn your family beforehand, then turn off your cell phone for a day. Better still, leave it on the night-stand so you won't be tempted to press "On."

Free-Range Brave Step: Do that list exercise the shrinks endorse. Think of one activity you did as a child that you are unwilling to let your own sweetheart do at the same age (baby-sitting, biking to a friend's), and make a list of twenty things that could conceivably go wrong. If there are any worries that strike you as realistic, help your child prepare for them. Teach your baby-sitter basic first aid. Teach your biker how to signal his turns. You'll feel better because you've helped them and *they've* demonstrated they're ready.

Giant Leap for Free-Range Kind: Try to actually think about fate. It's a hard concept to deal with, but if you can make peace with the idea that we cannot control everything that happens in life, you will feel less personally responsible for every breath your child takes, and you will be able to breathe easier, too. I'm not saying you don't need to take care of your children and prepare them for life (see above!). I'm saying you need to remember that you are not God. Or even Bobo.

Relax

Not Every Little Thing You Do Has That Much Impact on Your Child's Development

"**I** wonder how badly I will screw up my kids," begins a post on a parenting blog. "I know my kids will blame me for something. Pushing too much, or not enough. Being too strict or not playing with them enough, or how they want. Man, there are so many things they may have issues because of. Maybe instead of a college fund, we should start saving for a therapy fund."

Or maybe we should just shoot ourselves.

Sorry—that's just what it sounds like a lot of the time when parents start stewing about the job they're doing. So many of us are sure that despite our best intentions, we're making bad decisions that will have bad repercussions that will result in bad childhoods that will lead to bad adulthoods because we're bad. Please note the operative word in all this. It is not "good."

But is it really necessary for children to have an ideal child-hood? That they be raised by a set of sterling, intensely hands-on parents who do everything just right at every stage of the game, even as they read all seven volumes of Harry Potter out loud (with funny voices)?

God no. Think of all the happy, successful people who did not have that "perfect" childhood. Barack Obama's dad abandoned the family. Ronald Reagan's father was an alcoholic who kept losing jobs. On the nonpolitical, personal heroine side, Julie Andrews's mom was an alcoholic, too, with the added surprise of one day telling Julie: That man you think is your father—isn't.

And on and on and on.

This is not to suggest that if you want to raise a superstar you'd better throw a red-hot monkey wrench into their childhood. Just that there's a lot more leeway than we think when it comes to raising good kids. Or even great ones.

The whole Free-Range idea is that the twin notions of constant supervision and perfect parenting are not necessary. Obsessing about every emotional, intellectual, and psychological boost we could give our kids is not necessary. Even being 100 percent Free Range is not necessary. Our kids are not solely formed by our input, nor will they be irreparably harmed by our bumbling oh-so-humanly along.

So relax.

"Where I live, they lay such a trip on you about how you have to have dinner with your kids every night," says a mom in the suburbs of Washington, D.C. "The schools are telling us that families who eat together have children who are less prone to getting into trouble. So if anything bad happens, it's because you didn't sit down to dinner with them. I'll tell you it's a huge issue for me because I'm a single mother, and I have a rather taciturn son who's sixteen, and he's always had a sort of chip on his shoulder." Is it because she's divorced, this mom wonders? Or because she can't make it home to dinner every single night?

Well, if either of those were really what makes a person taciturn, Obama should be a sullen slacker. But he's not. Because we are not just the results of how our parents raised us. (Or left at age two and didn't raise us.) And even though it feels as though our children are ours to make or break—and it certainly sounds that way from all the advice we get from magazines and TV—a growing cadre of anthropologists, psychologists, biologists, educators, and all-around child development types are saying it ain't necessarily so. Yes, we parents have a lot of influence over our kids. But so do their friends, so do their siblings, so does their environment, and, especially, so do their genes.

"There's evidence for so much genetic influence in determining what children are like," says Kirsten Condry, an assistant professor of psychology at the Rochester Institute of Technology. "It's going to be amazing the number of things that turn out to have a genetic component to them."

You don't have to look very far to see how genes, rather than parenting styles, influence children. Try this simple three-part experiment:

Part I: Have or adopt a child and see how your amazing empathy and good cheer turn him into a bouncing bundle of smiles. Or, alternatively, watch how all your pathetic neuroses turn him into a total pain. See? You and your behavior created a particular type of child.

Part II: Have or adopt a second child. See how your amazing empathy has no visible effect on this constant whiner. Or watch how your pathetic neuroses just can't seem to upset your bouncing bundle of smiles.

Part III: Give 'em another hug and just do your best.

"Certainly kids learn how to be human from their parents, and what is expected of them. But all these fascinating differences among people don't come from parents," says Condry. "You can't say, 'Oh, if every parent does this, they will get the same child out or this behavior or that.' Even with the same input, children are fundamentally different."

Maybe that's not a big news flash: Children Born Different! But when we worry about getting every little aspect of child rearing "right"—the right snacks, the right toys, the right amount of TV time (my personal bugaboo)—we forget the bigger picture, which is that individually, these decisions don't end up mattering that much. And possibly even collectively they don't end up mattering quite that much.

Whenever I hear a mom or dad copping to some parental lapse and saying, only half jokingly, "I'm sure she'll be talking to her shrink about it in twenty years," I want to say, "If she does, it's not your fault! She is who she is!"

Personally, I spent years in therapy—really helpful ones—but I don't think it's because my loving parents raised me wrong. I think it's because I was born with the same glum, self-berating outlook as my mom and needed help realizing how not terrible I am. (Then I put my son on the subway and—surprise! Everyone told me how terrible I am. Back to square one.)

Judith Rich Harris made a huge splash a few years ago with her book *The Nurture Assumption*. It questioned whether parents have much of an impact on their children's development *at all*. Harris had been, of all things, a child development textbook writer. She wrote chapter after chapter on every which way parents bond (or don't) with their children, and how this shapes (or ruins) them, until one day she realized that she didn't believe a word she was writing. If children really get their entire way of dealing with life almost undiluted from their parents, she wondered, how could we explain something as simple as the fact that the children of immigrants speak the local language accent-free—and *better* than their parents? Clearly, kids pick up language from people other than mom and dad. Language is so crucial and basic that Harris realized kids probably pick up a lot of other crucial and basic characteristics too. Peers as well as parents are responsible for shaping the child.

Meantime, here was her other big realization: when we see the calm, quiet children of calm, quiet parents, we tend to assume that those parents used their superior parenting skills to make their children placid too. Lucky them. But isn't it just as possible that those calm, quiet parents had calm, quiet genes that they passed down, and that's the secret? How can we ever untangle what is nature and what is nurture?

One way, of course, is to look at twins, which Harris does. She finds one set of identical twins reared apart, both named Jim, who both "enjoyed woodworking, drove the same model Chevrolet, smoked Salems and drank Miller Lite." They both named their sons James Alan (well, one of them put a second *l* in Alan), and they were both volunteer firefighters.

Harris found another set of twins, one who was raised by his Catholic grandma in Germany, and one who was raised by his Jewish dad in Trinidad. Both of them flush the toilet before they go to the bathroom. Both read magazines from back to front. When they met for the first time, they were both wearing wire-rim glasses, short mustaches, and blue double-pocket shirts with epaulettes. It sounds like they were not only identical twins, they were identical dorks.

The chances of their parents in separate countries deliberately raising them both to be this dorky? Pretty slim. They got the dork gene from birth.

It is only in the last century or so that we started to believe that parenting, especially during the first few years of life, determines how a child turns out. A survey of Parisian moms back in 1780 found that 95 percent of them farmed their babies out to wet nurses—that is, to other women who would take in their babies and breastfeed them until the parents picked them up when they were weaned. Oftentimes, the moms didn't even visit very much. The idea that that first year was a crucial time for a child's intellectual development (not to mention bonding) was unheard of. For most of human history, parents believed a baby needed milk and a place to sleep, not, as many of us believe today, board books, soft books, story tapes, light-up rattles, and musical mobiles playing Mozart. Even Mozart didn't grow up hearing Mozart. (But his kids did, and whoever heard of them?)

Then along came Freud, who delved deep into childhood memories and found the root of a lot of our adult "issues" buried there. Freud revolutionized the way we look at parenting, because he saw children as blank pages that parents could, however unintentionally, scribble all over and crumple and tear and then, for good measure, use to wipe up spills. Or at least that is how his ideas have filtered down to pop culture.

Freud was a genius—who could deny his idea of the unconscious? Even unconsciously? But his theories had the unforeseen consequence of making parents very worried that a harsh word, a lack of encouragement, or even the opposite—extra-high hopes—could cause a child a lifetime of resentment and pain. It made parenting seem like a completely daunting, almost unnatural act. You had to be on guard all the time, lest you accidentally squash the emerging psyche.

These days, we buy into two basic assumptions. One, that children are wet clay at birth and dry out pretty fast, so we'd better sculpt them into something really good, really fast, or we'll be left with a lump. And two, that for some reason our children need more attention than any other generation, ever, if they are going to end up smart, well adjusted, and successful.

Let's examine the early childhood assumption first.

"If neuroscience has taught us anything, it's that people are resilient and they can learn across the life span," says John Bruer, president of the James S. McDonnell Foundation and author of *The Myth of the First Three Years*. Although a little baby is indeed ready to learn language and expressions and how the world works, that does not mean it needs to have everything crammed into its cranium before the gate slams shut at age four. So when parents worry that they'd better teach their kids the alphabet or their colors or any of the info you can find on, ugh, a Baby Einstein educational placemat (lest your child waste crucial learning minutes idly waiting for his Cheerios), that's just wrong.

"There's this crazy notion that we can affect brain development," says Kathy Hirsh-Pasek, director of the Temple University Infant Language Laboratory and coauthor of *Einstein Never Used Flash Cards*. Parents who think that teaching their child this or that skill ahead of the game or giving them the right educational tape or puzzle will make their children brainier have bought into a false worldview.

"Everywhere we've looked, the children are not gaining any advantages from these extra edutainment activities," says Hirsh-Pasek. So long as your child is not deprived of normal stimulation—that is, you don't lock him in a toy chest (even with educational toys!)—his brain is going to develop just fine.

So now let's look at how your parenting *does* affect your child.

Naturally, the environment you give her is going to have some bearing on the person she becomes. If she grows up in a house with a lot of books, it's more likely she'll be a reader than if she never encountered one. If she grows up in a home where all the girls learn to sew, she'll learn to sew too. But will this be her passion? Will she be great at it? All you can do is expose your kids to things you love and believe in.

In our home, we are raising one son who is crazy about manga—those Japanese comic books with all the swords and slashing. My husband and I had never seen manga till he brought it home. We are raising another son who is crazy about football. My husband and I had never watched football till he turned it on. We exposed them to literature and music. They fell for violent comics and guys ramming into each other. Like I said: we do not make our kids into who they are.

That doesn't mean we can hurt them or abuse them without consequence, obviously. So please don't. It just means that we don't have to hover so much and fret about our every parenting move. The small stuff is not worth the sweating, and maybe not the medium stuff either.

Why, then, do so many of us find ourselves worrying whether we're doing the right thing by our kids with each Chiclet-sized decision we make? It's not just the influence of therapy and talk TV. A big new influence is the Internet.

"The thing that blows me away is how judgmental these mothers are," says Hara Estroff Marano, author of *A Nation of Wimps*. She's talking about the mothers on mommy (and sometimes daddy) Web sites, who delight in taking potshots at each others' parenting.

The rise of these sites began in the mid-nineties, notes Marano, which dovetails almost precisely with the spike in helicopter parenting. *Quel* coincidence. Take a look at a typical exchange on a popular blog called Urban Baby and you'll see how Internet, inter-parent swiping provided this movement with its rocket fuel:

One mom—call her Bea—writes, out of the blue: "It's the formula that makes all these children obese. They get addicted to the sugar young. You don't see many long-term breastfed children who are obese."

This is the equivalent of throwing a bucket of Kentucky Fried mice into the cat wing of the local pound.

"I was a formula baby and I have been thin my entire adult life: 5'7" and 105," a mom writes back, unable to resist the bait.

"Topic is fat kids, not thin, defensive adults," zings another.

"Actually, topic is whether formula-fed babies are automatically obese, not your pathetic need to snark."

Back and forth, back and forth:

"Eat something, you defensive anorexic."

"This is stupid! Many kids are formula fed and not obese!"

"But most obese children are formula fed."

God, who *cares* what other people's kids are fed? Why are they even discussing this? Finally, one lady tells Bea that if she feels so strongly about it, why doesn't she just go donate her breast milk? Bea responds that she already did. Take *that*.

You might think that would be the end of it, but one more mom sputters that Bea is a "looser."

Breasty Bea says, "Learn to spell if you are going to attack."

"Don't waste time spell checking," the attacker tells her. "Get to work bottling up that boob milk!"

All the women in this exchange are now ready to clobber each other with high chairs. It's like World Wrestling for lactating moms. And what we have just witnessed repeats itself over and over, all day long: parents who only want to do what's right—no one was proposing bringing up baby on Mai Tais, after all—are now at each other's throats. And breasts. The idea that, formula fed or not, most kids turn out fine does not occur to them.

No wonder parents feel so insecure and second-guessed all the time. Someone is always second-guessing! And usually those some-ones can find a study or expert that supports their side. It's as if parenting has become the topic at a huge, nationwide debate tour-nament. And that's exactly the problem: too much focus.

"Children just used to be seen as a part of life," says Nancy Mc-Dermott, a parenting blogger on the British Web site Spiked. They were something you had, not something that defined you. Now? They're like publicly available report cards, documenting all our parental successes and failures. They embody our beliefs and who we are.

I'm pretty sure that's why the media are so obsessed with celebrity parents, and never let up on the hunt for that holy tabloid grail: a star's "baby bump." Is it there? Is it bigger than last week? Is it *twins*? The tabloids are just mirroring society's obses-sion with parenthood, from the moment of conception (was it IVF?) onward. So now Angelina Jolie isn't first and foremost a movie star. She's a mega mama who happens to be an actress.

"Jolie's new family has come to define her," writes *USA Today*. Yeah, we noticed. She's got about seventeen kids. Pictures of Jolie in *W* magazine show her breastfeeding. Can you imagine a movie star from any other era—Ava Gardner, Audrey Hepburn, even Jane Fonda—posing *in flagrante parentis* like that? Of course not. But that was before parenthood became the pinnacle of accomplishment.

Being defined by our role as parents not only makes the "job" seem bigger but also presents a potential pitfall (or, if you're Angelina, a Pitt-fall): we'd better be doing a great job. Everyone's watching! And that's where the exaggerated worry and fear come in.

"One reason parents feel under so much pressure to get their kids into the 'right' school and do all these things is because parents' esteem is really bound up with their parenting," says McDermott. It's my child/my self. Or, as Laura Schlesinger, host of a super-successful radio talk show, so irritatingly introduces herself: "I am my kid's mom."

Because "mom" and "dad" have become such public roles, the public feels free to weigh in on parenting subjects that used to be private. Whether we feed our kids Fritos. Whether we hire tutors.

Was yours a vaginal delivery, boss? And, of course, whether we are watching our children closely enough.

Free-Range Parents try to resist this kind of constant carping and comparing, even as they remember there is no one right way to raise a kid. There's not even one right way to figure out whether or not that kid should have a donut. In theory, knowing that most of our decisions don't matter all that much should help us relax, as should realizing how much of a child's fate is determined by his genes anyway.

So when you find yourself wondering, "WWAD?"—What Would (perfect, beautiful, constantly breastfeeding) Angelina Do? Ask yourself this instead: "WWIDIIJSWTICRMKRHAN?" ("What Would I Do If I Just Stopped Worrying That I Could Ruin My Kid Right Here and Now?")

Maybe we need a catchier slogan. But I think you get the idea.

REAL WORLD

If You're Sick of Playing Patty-Cake ...

You may think one of your jobs as a parent is to get down on your hands and knees and play with your children, no matter how exhausted you are, because they need the "stimulation." But as anthropologist David Lancy discovered, a lot of the rest of the world finds this utterly bizarre. In most non-Western societies, the idea of parents playing baby games is as wacky as parents eating baby food.

As recently as 1914, this was the official view in the United States, too, with a government pamphlet urging mothers *not* to play with their children, lest they overexcite them.

So if you're sick of playing patty-cake but think you'd better keep patting or the dullard you create may be your own, it seems that history and the rest of the world are willing to give you a pass.

Going Free Range

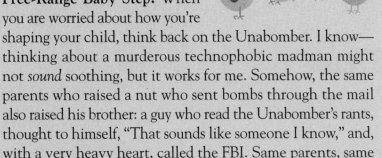

Free-Range Baby Step: When you are worried about how you're shaping your child, think back on the Unabomber. I know— thinking about a murderous technophobic madman might not *sound* soothing, but it works for me. Somehow, the same parents who raised a nut who sent bombs through the mail also raised his brother: a guy who read the Unabomber's rants, thought to himself, "That sounds like someone I know," and, with a very heavy heart, called the FBI. Same parents, same house. Clearly, there is more at work on our kids than how we raise them. (All right—if you don't want to think about the Unabomber, think about the Baldwin boys. One's a born-again Christian, and one is Alec.)

Free-Range Brave Step: Visit relatives or friends who are raising their kids in a way you abhor. Maybe the fridge is filled with junk food, or the children are forbidden to watch *The Simpsons*. Talk to those kids one-on-one and see if you can't find a shred of humanity left in them despite their parents' best efforts. You will.

Giant Leap for Free-Range Kind: If you're really worried that your actions are going to screw your kids up and send them straight to therapy, beat them to the punch. Go there first. Get yourself a shrink and talk about your fears and inadequacies. Not only will you feel better, but by the time you're done and can really relax, your kids will be grown and out the door anyway.

Fail!

It's the New Succeed

Stephen Haberman edges close to the stranger's car and looks up the street. He looks down the street. No one is watching the sixty-five-year-old grandpa, so as best as he can, he yanks off the bumper sticker MY CHILD IS AN HONOR STUDENT AT . . .

Nowhere! Not anymore. The big brag has been torn off.

Call it guerilla therapy.

"I think it's a bad thing to do to kids," says the Dallas psychotherapist about the stickers. "It says to the child, your value is this grade average, and your job is to do things that will please me and make me look good so I can put a bumper sticker on my car."

It is not a child's job to make her parents look good, and it is not a parent's job to make her child look good. Both of them have the responsibility to do the best they can, and when that's not good enough, to fail.

A responsibility to fail? Yup.

Failure isn't very popular, especially when you live in a society geared not just for success but for super-success, like "Harvard" or "Thoracic Surgeon." Or, better yet, "Harvard Thoracic Surgeon (and Part-Time Sex Columnist)." The same society that decided a couple of decades ago that everyone should wear brand names all over their clothes also decided along the way that only brand-name colleges will do. Polo, Nike, Princeton, Brown. Same deal. Instant confirmation of one's worth. That's why a ninety-second video called "Big Failures" went viral last year. It was the equivalent of mooning our success-obsessed culture.

As the camera pans a typical schoolroom in this mini-film, a man's voice intones: "A teacher told him he was too stupid to learn anything and he should go into a field where he could succeed by virtue of his pleasant personality. *(Pause.)* Thomas Edison." The man's voice continues: "His fiancée died, he failed in business twice, he had a nervous breakdown, and was defeated in eight elections." A penny spins around to reveal *(pause)* "Abraham Lincoln." Now we see a high school gym. "Cut from his high school basketball team, he went home, locked himself in his room, and cried." It was *(pause)* Michael Jordan, naturally, and the *(pause)* Beatles were turned down by Decca Records because their music wasn't catchy and guitars were old hat. The video, by a company called Bluefishtv on the site Wimp.com, concludes, "Life = Risk." Then it shows a little boy riding his bike down the street.

"He should fall," said my husband.

But the boy doesn't. Even the folks who make videos about failure know how hard it is to watch in real life, especially when it happens to a kid. But the whole point is that if you're not willing to fall, you're not going to learn how to ride a bike.

Why, then, is failure such a taboo topic when it comes to our own kids? We all know it's part of life. We know it builds character. Why, to get straight to the point bothering *me*, do I feel guilty for letting my older son, Morry, quit electric guitar after just three months, and then letting his younger brother, Izzy, do the same thing after three long years of piano?

Because parents are supposed to encourage their kids to succeed, that's why. Let them discover their inner Hendrix/Horowitz (after years of us exclaiming, "Why aren't you practicing!!!?") Quitters never win, and . . . we quit.

"Is there a rule that says your child has to play soccer or piano?" asked psychiatrist Alvin Rosenfeld, coauthor of *The Over-Scheduled Child*, when I told him my parental sins. "I don't think they're any more required than jai alai," he said. "A lot of times parents say,

'You have to put up with this torture for some time in the future when you'll appreciate it.' But do they say, 'Marry this guy. It's going to be torture for seventeen years, but then it's going to be good'? It's a silly notion. It's puritanical."

Wow! A well-respected shrink is on the record saying you can let your kids up and quit something they're not good at—or just plain hate—and it's not the end of the world. *They* can fail at the activity, *you* can fail at producing a prodigy. Or even a child who can plunk out "Für Elise."

So why does that reasonable attitude feel too easy to be right? Blame our wiring.

Parents come pretty much preprogrammed to help their children survive. We feed our progeny, shelter them, teach them. And back when their survival depended on outrunning hungry hyenas, we'd shout, "Don't quit! Atta boy! Show 'em what you're made of! Run!" Because when atta boy didn't run quite fast enough, it was a pretty crushing defeat. The hyenas went home with the trophy, if you catch my drift.

Unfortunately, that same deep desire to preserve our young from death and dismemberment is what we now bring to the SATs. "That preservation mechanism is good for survival, but it has a very sensitive trigger," says psychologist Wendy Grolnick, coauthor of *Pressured Parents, Stressed-Out Kids*. "And these days it's set off all the time, because we are getting cues that say, 'Your child is in trouble! Your child is going to fail! Your child is not going to make that play, that soccer team. Your child is not going to be able to get into that magnet program!'"

The cues come from guidance counselors, from test prep brochures, from ads that appear when a baby is born and hint that if you don't sign up for a mommy-baby bouncy ball class, *fast*, your kid can kiss that hand-eye coordination (and MLB contract) goodbye. Hungry hyenas have been replaced by their modern-day equivalent: mere averageness. Mediocrity is nipping at our children's heels, and if they ever trip or fall, our current culture delights in warning us, their future is grim indeed.

This fear for our children is so visceral that it actually causes heart palpitations and sweating and all the other physical symptoms of panic and grief. It's the wave of nausea that crashes over you when you hear the other parents talking about the play their children in the "gifted" third-grade class are writing while your child's third-grade class is scheduled to sing the Band-Aid jingle. The anxiety lasts all throughout childhood because the goal of "survival to adulthood" has morphed into "getting into a good college." However far off it looms, college admission is the ultimate source of our emphasis on achievement—and our attendant fear of failure.

"Please list your principal extracurricular, volunteer and family activities and hobbies in the order of their interest to you," reads the Common Application—an online college application accepted by many colleges. "Include specific events and/or major accomplishments such as musical instrument played, varsity letters earned, etc."

Surely your seventeen-year-old has plenty of "major accomplishments" to list? Not that most of us adults do (how's that cancer cure coming?), but there are *seven* empty lines for your child to fill with *seven* different activities, including "positions held, honors won or letters earned." Don't tell me your kid just comes home and draws all afternoon, Mrs. da Vinci!

"I blame the admissions process for the overpressured situation we're in," says Emily Glickman, who should know. She's president of Abacus Guide Educational Consulting, and her job is helping New York City parents find a good private school match for their kids. Every day, she watches how the schools' exponential expectations are driving parents nuts. "People are always blaming so-called helicopter parents, but if you think about it, private schools and colleges are asking so much from our kids. Even to get into kindergarten, it's good to have a resume."

What could possibly be on a four-year-old's resume—besides applesauce?

"That you've taken art classes, that you're good at sports, that you've done well on the ERB," the entrance exam for private schools, Glickman says.

Clearly, private preschools in Manhattan are the perfect petri dish for parental hysteria, but as go preppy tots in their Prada party shoes, so go the rest of us in our Payless sneakers, eventually. Plenty of public schools have gifted tracks starting in kindergarten, and the path leads right on up through high school AP classes. Woe to the child who develops a good pencil grip at age seven instead of four. She may already have missed the chance to get into the tippy-top elementary school program, which leads to the best middle and high school programs, which, of course, lead to the Ivy League–level colleges. Or at least that is the perception.

Each step of the way, kids either succeed—or fail. And success is defined as being solidly Lake Woebegon "above average" in all the classes and extracurriculars that will fill those slots on the college application. How can you possibly make your kid that successful?

Jill Besnoy, a mom in New Jersey, is mulling over that right now. Her son is approaching a major turning point in his sports career: Should he join the swim team?

The coach would like her son to get serious about the sport. "But the swim team is four days a week, and that doesn't include the swim meets on the weekend," says Besnoy. A schedule like that would take time away from his tennis and soccer—two other areas of strength. How can she be sure he is ready to commit to a swimming career?

After all, he's only six.

That sounds silly, of course, but it's happening all the time. Besnoy is surrounded by other parents making just such choices for their first graders. They feel pressured to choose activities in which their tykes can wildly succeed. One of her son's friends plays ice hockey five days a week. Most likely his parents hope that excelling in a sport will lead to other opportunities for their boy—a college scholarship, or at least admission to a "good" school.

"Parents want to send their kids to every enriching activity because the schools have set it up that way," says Glickman. A kid applying to college saying, "I play some sports, and like writing, but

I haven't won any prizes or anything," is like a kid showing up for the college tour naked. It's just not done. They have to show up with accomplishments, which is why, when they fail at those, parents often despair.

But here's one who didn't. "I am, by Washington D.C. standards, a failure as a parent," Welmoed Sisson, a stay-at-home mom, wrote to me. "My kids didn't play on sports teams. We never signed them up for anything they didn't ask for. They haven't gone to New Orleans to rebuild houses or anything else to pad their college applications. They both went to the local public high school. They get good but not stellar grades. And not only did I neglect to send my kids to SAT prep classes, I didn't push them to take the SATs more than once." At the moment, Sisson's nineteen-year-old son is in community college, "because he doesn't know yet what he wants to do with his life." And her daughter, a high school senior, applied to only one college. Her parents did not read her application.

This is so beyond the norm for our generation's hands-on parents that I had to call Sisson to find out what was going on.

"People are astounded that I'm not intervening more," she admitted. "I just believe in my kids." She's not a slacker mom—she read to her children almost every night, even into their teens. But she and her husband let them follow their own interests. (And drop out of piano!) As a result, her son is now studying computer game design even as he works part-time selling shoes, and her daughter wants to become a zoologist or animal behaviorist. They have the same ambitious dreams as other kids. They're just not as worried about getting there in an Ivy League limo.

"My friends occasionally say, 'You're not going to get into the college you want!' but I disagree," says Diana, the Sisson's seventeen-year-old. The college she wants to attend has a working farm (she does part-time farm work already), and on one of her essays she spent six paragraphs explaining that if she doesn't get in, she will reapply for the rest of her life until she does.

That very outlook—"If I fail, so what? I will try again"—turns out to be exactly what some psychologists say is the surest path to success.

Carol Dweck, author of *Mindset: The New Psychology of Success*, has won a lot of attention, even from the folks at Apple, for her work on failure, success, and how they are linked. This interest was born out of her own experience as a child in grammar school, when one of her teachers seated her students front to back, according to their IQ scores. Lovely.

Dweck happened to be in seat 1, but this was no comfort to her. Being dubbed an official "success" by virtue of a test meant that she was only as good as her next score. Rather than feeling proud and fearless, she felt poised for a fall. As for the kids in the back row—the officially designated dummies—it couldn't have been too great for them, either.

Eventually Dweck's studies led her to the belief that there are two kinds of mindsets. She refers to the first as the "fixed" mindset, that of the folks who believe that they are innately intelligent or good at something. These people end up fearing challenges, because if they fail, it is a blow to their entire sense of self. After all, they defined themselves as smart, then a test showed they aren't! The only logical conclusion is that they must actually be dumb—they think. So rather than trying to scale new heights (or take new tests), the "fixed" folks spend a lot of time trying to avoid potential failures and maintain their status quo. No leaps for them.

Then there are the folks—and it sounds like the Sissons somehow raised two—who see failure in less drastic terms. If they fail at something, it just means they have to learn or try something new so they can do better the next time. This is what Dweck calls the "expandable" or "growth" mindset.

The good news is that it may be possible to teach the growth mindset, if we remind kids, and ourselves, that the mind is a muscle. It can be challenged, it can stretch, it can get better the same way an athlete can get better, by practicing and stumbling and fumbling along the way. As Thomas Edison said when asked how it felt to fail so many times, "I have not failed. I've just found 10,000 ways that won't work."

Call it whatever you want, Tom, failing allows for a chance to try again. But it also allows for something else, just as valuable: the chance for a child (or adult) to call it quits and go in an entirely new direction.

Celeste Brooks's son Michael started soccer at age five, but by sixth grade, he was a benchwarmer. His mom, who happens to work at his Virginia school, told him: Practice more or you won't make the seventh-grade team.

Well, he didn't and he didn't, and his mom's friends were shocked when she didn't pull any strings to fix that, either. She just let him fail and then watched as he dusted himself off (not a one-day affair) and switched his allegiances to track. Now he not only loves that sport but also is much better at it. I must say that exactly the same scenario played out with my own soccer-to-track nephew in suburban Chicago and with other kids I know, too: they failed and floundered, only to be reborn as something else.

And we're not just talking about rebirth in after-school sports. There are all sorts of fields to fail in, including good ol' life skills. Then you can be reborn as someone more responsible. Michigan mother of four Marybeth Hicks actively looks for opportunities for her children to fail. "Forgotten your homework? Left the trombone at home? Forgot that it's a 'free dress day'?" the *Bringing Up Geeks* author chuckles. For kids in uniforms at Catholic school, that's a mistake of Dante-esque proportions.

Nonetheless, Hicks refuses to hop in the car to make things right—not just because she wants her kids to do better the next time (sometimes they do, sometimes they don't), but also because she doesn't want to have to drive anywhere before she's showered.

Totally legit! One thing we parents forget is that in our desire to keep our kids from failing, we sometimes fail ourselves or our spouses. We're off to deliver the left-at-home shin guards or science posters, and pretty soon there's no time left for anything or anyone else. What's your own social life (or marriage!)—chopped liver? Wrap it up in a brown paper bag and race it over to yourself! Eat it in bed with the one you love! Hicks says she feels bad whenever she fails to ease up on herself and let her children fail.

Not that failure is the ultimate goal. Aside from helping us learn painful lessons or change our boneheaded focus, once in a while failure can deliver a much sweeter surprise: flat-out success.

As a high school student, Adryenn Ashley lived for cheerleading. In fact, the California girl lived for it so much that during any semester she wasn't on the cheerleading squad, she skipped her classes. The second semester of her junior year was like that, but she did show up in the fall to try out for the senior cheerleading team, the Song Leaders.

She was great. She rocked! After all, all she'd done with her hooky time was practice cheers. But she didn't make the cut because her grades were too low.

That's failure.

So she dropped out of high school.

That's failure with a capital F.

Not long afterward, she enrolled in the College of Marin, a community college. And what did she do there? "I started the cheerleading program!" says Ashley. "They didn't have one. It's still there to this day—and I'm forty."

She's also, by the way, a published author and owner of her own business, WOW! Is Me. (Yes, it does sound a little like a cheer.) And, for the record, she helped chair her high school's reunion.

Ever year, Stephen Haberman, the bumper-sticker-peeling shrink, is called in to give a chat to Ashley's exact opposites: the high achievers at one of the Dallas high schools near him. It always ends up emotional. "They complain that they're not able to sleep; they talk about irregular heartbeats. You start doing a little simple relaxation stress management thing, and they begin to cry. It's so sad! We've got a school system where a perfect grade-point average is 4.0, but if you take advanced classes you get 4.6 or 4.7—how crazy is that?"

So why not tell them the truth: "It's OK to fail, at least a little bit?"

"They'd never have me back!" says Haberman. "You can't tell a child it's OK to fail if it's not OK with the parents to fail. So you've got to stop thinking in terms of *failure*. Making a choice about doing less of this stuff is not 'failure.' It's being successful in making a choice about how you're going to live your life. 'Failure' is scary. It's the boogey man."

He's got a point. So maybe let's think of Commandment 12 as really, "Believe in your kids and that they'll be fine even if they don't join the swim team at age six."

And maybe even if they quit their music lessons.

REAL (ISH) WORLD

Lessons from "Little Miss Sunshine"

Garrett Peck of Arlington, Virginia, got to thinking about this movie. If you haven't seen it, don't read this. If you have, do:

> *Little Miss Sunshine* has this wonderful theme stitched throughout it of what it means to fail. Every one of the characters fails at what they want to accomplish: Olive fails to become the Little Miss Sunshine. Her dad fails to get his book published. Her mom is living in a dysfunctional marriage. Her brother realizes he's color-blind and can't fly Navy jets. Her gay uncle loses his partner, gets demoted to the #2 Proust scholar in the country, is fired from his teaching position, and fails to commit suicide! And the grandfather, well, he dies of a heroin overdose.
>
> And yet at the end, there is an incredible feeling of resiliency in this family, that despite all of their failures, you knew they were going to make it. The grandfather, played by Alan Arkin, told Olive on the night he died that a loser is someone who is too scared to even try. That, in a nutshell, is the key point of the movie. We all fail, but that doesn't make us losers. Resiliency is about picking ourselves up and getting back in the game after a failure.

Going Free Range

Free-Range Baby Step: Peel any bragging bumper stickers off your car. Explain to your child, "It's not because I don't love you. It's because I do."

Free-Range Brave Step: Watch that failure video: http://wimp.com/bigfailures. Think about some of the things you failed at and how, if you had succeeded, you wouldn't have something you love today. (Personal confession: I didn't get into Harvard. First choice. Yes, maybe that's why I keep trying to make fun of it. Sue me. Point is, if I'd gone there, I never would have met my husband or had my darling kids, who'll never get into Harvard because they don't play an instrument, etc., etc. So hooray for failure . . . pretty much.)

Giant Leap for Free-Range Kind: Find one thing you've pushed your kids to do that they don't really like and aren't good at, and let them drop it. Be prepared for cheers.

Commandment 13

Lock Them Out

Make Them Play — or Else!

You want your children to be smart, sweet, social, successful, creative, curious, kind, and unfat. Do you:

A. Sign them up for karate?

B. Have them try out for *Hairspray*?

C. Hire that highly recommended tutor who will arm wrestle them until they recite their times tables, then take them outside for triathlon training in ankle weights?

D. Just let them play?

Well, if you know anything about the latest, greatest findings about childhood—or even how rhetorical questions are generally posed in quiz form—you know it's D. Play.

Play turns out to be so stunningly essential to childhood, it's like love, sunshine, and broccoli all juiced together. It is the key to all the things we dearly hope our schools are teaching our kids (but secretly fear they're not), including basic math, communication skills, negotiation skills, leadership, a scientific outlook, fairness, flexibility, and physics. Yes, physics. You throw a baseball and learn about speed, force, and the physical properties of windows. Also sometimes the price of windows, too, so let's throw in economics. The run-around kind of play is good exercise. The sit-around kind of play is good for creativity.

Unfortunately—almost bizarrely—something this fun and formative and *free* is disappearing faster than polar bears in an Al Gore PowerPoint. In fact, that's the only reason I'm pleading for play right here. Go back a few generations and this would have been ridiculous. Play was the default setting of most kids. You didn't have to encourage them to do it, or convince their parents, "Please let your children cavort; it is oh-so developmentally worthwhile!" It was just a given: kids played. They had playtime in preschool, playtime after school, playtime during school.

Now? Not so much. In fact, in just the five years from 1997 to 2002, the amount of time the average six- to eight-year-old spends on creative play has declined by about a third, according to Susan Linn, whose book *The Case for Make Believe* is the bible on all of this. If you want to see what's going on play-wise with your own eyes (and it's not pitch dark outside), put down this book and walk around your neighborhood. Hellooooooo? Where are all the kids?

Not playing. At least, not playing outside with each other in that 3-D thing we call "reality." A recent survey of moms found that 70 percent of them played outside pretty much every day when they were growing up. But only 31 percent of their own children do. That's right: *fewer than a third of our kids are playing outside anymore*. Childhood has changed in less time that it takes to say, "Red rover, red rover . . . let's go inside and play Halo 3."

Who or what is to blame? Oh, pretty much every aspect of pop culture except Tina Fey. In no particular order, the play-killers are:

Standardized tests. In our quest to leave no child with a no. 2 pencil behind, our schools have been sacrificing recess and gym time, even in preschool, to allot more time for reading, writing, and math. Nothing wrong with those subjects, of course, but they go down a lot easier when kids have had a chance to play. And I know some kids (one of them in my living room right now) who would look a lot less as if they were heading off to lethal injection each morning if they knew there was going to be double recess at school.

Abduction fear. This one is really off base. As I've said before, if you look at the statistics gathered by the government, you will find that crimes against children are actually plummeting. From 1993 to 2004 the rate of aggravated assaults against kids went down 74 percent. Sexual assaults went down even more. I don't think you could ask for more wonderful news about crime. Yet we are more worried about it than ever, so we don't let our kids go outside and play. Instead they stay inside, either doing heaps of homework (see test prep, above), or enjoying their . . .

Electronics. What can I say? Electronics are incredibly seductive. We had to install a program that automatically turns off the PC after a certain amount of time, or our kids might never eat or sleep or—anything. I was worried they'd end up like that astronaut with the diapers. Why waste time away from the computer? Kids are spending so much time in front of one screen or another that one study found that 40 percent of children *age three months or younger* are already regular TV watchers. (This, despite the American Academy of Pediatrics's recommendation of no screen time at all before age two.) It's really hard to get up and go out, especially to a neighborhood devoid of kids, when there's already an entire electronic world ready to entertain and play with you. And speaking of entertaining electronics, the most ironic antiplay force turns out to be . . .

Elmo! Well, not just Elmo. But that *Sesame Street* shill is a lot less innocent than he appears. How could something as cute as Elmo be killing play? Easy. He is one of the vast army of "Look at me" toys—toys that basically function in the same way as a TV screen. They are there to be passively consumed. When a kid presses the button, Elmo sings or dances or laughs himself silly.

Who's having all the fun?

You'd think that because the little red guy hails from an educational TV show, he must be an educational toy. And in a way, he is: he's educating kids to sit there and press a button and wait for something entertaining to happen. It's an easy lesson to learn—but it's the opposite of play.

Organized activities. I don't want to sound like an absolute killjoy—especially when I'm here trying to resuscitate joy—but organized activities have also cut down on old-fashioned play. Not that these activities don't have a lot going for them. They do. They can be fun and something to look forward to, and they teach kids a lot of cool things, from singing to skating to my childhood passion, rug hooking. (What can I say? It was the seventies.) In neighborhoods where it really is too dangerous to hang out at the local playground, organized activities are a godsend, keeping kids safe and social while offering them new interests. But the one thing that kids in supervised programs generally do not do, whether in the suburbs or the inner city, is just plain *play*. They follow instructions, they listen to the leader. It's like a pleasant form of school. But play turns out to be something almost totally different from that. And if we are going to try to wrest it away from all these powerful forces, we need to take a look at why we should even bother.

"You can take the play out of learning, but you can't take the learning out of play." That's what a Minnesota educator named Brock Dubbels likes to say, and it just about sums up what makes play so fun—and essential.

We spend a lot of time trying to fill our kids with valuable lessons, especially in the classroom, but we forget all the valuable lessons they can learn on their own, at the playground, out in nature, or even within the comfort of four cardboard walls.

Make-believe play actually teaches kids to think *outside* the you-know-what. The reason you always hear parents marveling, "I bought him that walking, talking, Star Trek mega death ray, but he was more interested in the box," is that the box *is* more interesting, in some ways (after one has pretended to shoot one's little brother several times with the mega death ray and sent him wailing from the room). When a kid has a box, it can be anything, right? A house, a castle, a cave. So already it's more flexible than most of today's fancy toys, which not only "do" things (like Elmo) but are also often tied to a movie or TV show. The problem with those licensed toys is that they come preprogrammed in a child's mind to do whatever the character does on TV or in the movies. You don't give Darth Vader a high-pitched squeaky voice if you already know exactly how he sounds. So creativity gets a bit crippled.

But a box—ah. It abides by the simple "good toy" principle, which is that it gives all the make-believe power to the kid. A good toy, they say, is 10 percent toy and 90 percent child. So, as Linn points out in my favorite example in her book, if your kid wants to be Harry Potter, he could make a wand from a stick or a straw. Magic! He has created something from almost nothing. Or you could give him an official Harry Potter Magic Wand—no imagination required.

Naturally, a lot of parents think it is far *better* to give him the "real" wand than to have him make do with a stick. (Which, admittedly, would look pretty cheap under the Christmas tree.) And, naturally, the kid thinks so too. So good-bye innovation—and thrift.

Unlike the stick or straw, however, the official wand is one thing and one thing only. So now when the child also wants a sword or an arrow, he believes he needs those "official" toys too. The stick could have been all of the above. The official wand is just an official wand. So good-bye flexibility and imagination. And thrift? Foiled again. (Come to think of it, tin foil is foiled again too.)

A ball is a "good toy" because a kid can play with it any which way. Ditto, paint. A basic doll is good because a child can decide if it's a nice doll or a naughty doll, or a crybaby or whatever. She uses her imagination. Therapists love toys like this in play therapy because if they see the kid screaming, "BAD DOLL! BAD DOLL!" for an hour or so, they suspect something's going on at home. Kids use these blank-slate toys to work out their problems, but also to become more patient and resourceful.

"A kid who can't get a sports car puts a bunch of pillows under the dining room table," says Dubbels. That kid has figured out how to satisfy himself without begging grandma for a $130,000 Toys R Us gift card. That's not a bad lesson to learn, right? If you can't get what you want, make do with what you have? So make-believe play increases patience, problem solving, and the ability to entertain oneself. It's worth its weight in batteries. And that's just when kids are playing *alone*.

Now let's look at what happens when kids play together. That's what Keith Sawyer, author of *Group Genius: The Creative Power of Collaboration*, did in a preschool for a year, using microphones to catch all the children's little mutterings and negotiations. At the sand table, said Sawyer, you might hear one child taking a toy giraffe and burying it. "He's dead."

Then the other kid, rather than bursting into tears or running away, announces, "Then there was an earthquake! And now the giraffe is alive again!" And she unburies the beloved toy.

They didn't come to blows over the fate of the giraffe. They came up with stories instead. Call these stories "narratives," and you'll realize that when they play, kids spontaneously work on the very lessons a whole lot of their school day is devoted to, such as writing. Moreover, this give-and-take among the kids is what grown-ups call "negotiation"—another good skill to have. Also involved is compromise, which is what you have to do when you want to play the all-powerful wicked witch and your friend wants to play all-powerful Batman. The witch cackles and threatens Batman. Batman flies from bed to bed and tries to scare the witch. (Impossible.) That's what Joel Barnett and I did after school for about a million years. Now I hear he's some super-successful real estate developer in suburban Chicago, and I'm sorry if I have just embarrassed him, but that's what witches do. Besides, he's a superhero, so he can take it. In any event, that kind of game made us compromise, communicate, create, negotiate, and jump around. It also honed my ability to cast spells. All good.

As we got older, the kids on my block got together for kickball games. And it turns out that in these run-around games—as opposed to make-believe games—a whole new set of skills come into play (so to speak).

"I grew up in the Bronx, and when I was eight or nine, I'd go out to the street corner and there were no adults and we'd have to be creative enough to come up with our own games," says John DeMatteo, thirty-four. He and his buddies would declare the telephone pole first base, or safety, or whatever, and then they'd play running bases or some new game they'd invent. They'd decide the rules, they'd change them if the game got dull, and, inevitably, they'd deal with disputes. "That kind of creative thinking is lost when adults are dictating what kids are doing every second," says DeMatteo. So it may be surprising to learn that he grew up to become one of those very adults who watch over kids as they play. He's a gym teacher.

However, he is a gym teacher who is already considered among the most innovative in New York City. The public middle school where he teaches is in Chinatown, across from a housing project, and it didn't have any after-school sports when he came on board six years ago. Now it has twenty-one sports and thirty-eight teams; 70 percent of the students participate, making his the largest middle school sports program in the city. And in 2007 he was invited to Hong Kong to work his magic, getting the sluggish kids there back into physical activity. How did he do this?

Same way he does it back home. He had them come up with their own games.

"In June, it's the last unit we have," says DeMatteo describing what happens at the Manhattan Academy of Technology, where he teaches. "I put them in teams, and they have to confer with each other. Then they come into class and teach their game to the rest of the class, and the whole class plays the game they came up with. A lot of the games are good enough that I've added them to my curriculum."

Such as? "Oh, we have a game, Capture the Farm Animal, that I don't think any adult in their right mind would have come up with. It's a combination of, like, four different games. They also play Football Frenzy, Tickle Ball, Ultimate Team Wall Ball, and games that haven't even been named yet." When he leads workshops for other gym teachers, DeMatteo teaches them those student-made games, which the visiting teachers then bring home to their own schools. But mostly they go back eager to get their own students doing what DeMatteo did as a child. Inventing games. Having fun. Being creative. Running around.

The running-around part goes a long way toward addressing another consequence of too much kid time spent sitting inside: obesity—a word that makes it sound as if "fat" is too dirty even to say. The fact is, our kids are getting fatter, and this is happening, curiously enough, right in tandem with the largest growth of childhood sports programs in history. What's different about most supervised sports programs as compared to kids just playing by themselves is that the playing kids seem to run around more. At my sons' old show-up-and-you-get-a-trophy baseball league, the coach spent the first fifteen minutes or so discussing good sportsmanship. After maybe an hour of play—with a lot of kids practically sleepwalking in the outfield because, barring a miracle, no ball would ever reach them—there was another fifteen-minute pep talk about how everyone's a winner. Even the losers. Especially the losers. The last ten minutes were devoted to nutritious snacks, on the assumption the kids would die if they ate a Chips Ahoy instead of well-washed grapes.

My kids barely worked up a sweat. But put them into a yard with their cousins playing, yes indeed, a made-up football game called Fumble-Roosky, and they tumble in with cheeks so rosy we have to run and get the camera.

We revere that kind of "real" fun because it's not always easy to get our kids outside. Put another way: it's almost always *hard* to get them outside. But we've started trying to make it a priority. Play gets everything going: the mind, the body, the will to live. It is so crucial to child health that the American Academy of Pediatrics wrote a landmark report on it a few years back, recommending that grown-ups stop adding hours to the school day and shrinking recess and supervising all childhood activities. It begged parents to remember that even if we desperately want our kids to "succeed," play does not take away from that pursuit. "As parents prepare their children for the future, they cannot know precisely which skills they will need for the workforce," wrote the docs. But confidence, competence, creativity, tenacity, fairness, decency, and the ability to have a little fun will surely help.

So will the ability to cast spells and vanquish superheroes as they jump from bed to bed. But kids are going to have to learn this on their own, as did I.

REAL WORLD

We Thought of Everything, Including Boards with Nails in Them to Fight off Alligators

Free-Range Parents push their kids to play and create on their own. But we still tune in to what's going on—and even intervene, when necessary. Here's an example from Pablo Solomon:

> I am now an internationally recognized artist living the good life. But as a kid, I lived in some of the poorest neighborhoods in Houston. So it was always a treat to spend time in the summers with my cousin who lived in the country. We would look for arrowheads and petrified wood. We would catch snakes and play with our chemistry sets.
>
> One summer when we were about nine years old, we decided to build a raft to go down the Brazos River to the Gulf of Mexico—about a 200-mile trip from near College Station. We worked and worked. We thought of everything, including boards with nails in them to fight off alligators. We had a storage box for our food and drinks. We were ready to launch. Of course, I expected my uncle to flip out and say, "You kids are crazy! You will sink and drown." Instead, he put our raft on a trailer and hauled it and us to the river.
>
> It was bigger than we remembered. And the current was going fast. We were a bit afraid, but could not chicken out

(continued on next page)

now. My uncle put life jackets on us, told us to get on the raft, and then he gave us a shove into the current. We were terrified and excited at the same time. We tried to control our raft with our homemade paddle with no luck! Just as we were beginning to panic, we realized that my uncle had tied a very long rope to our raft. He had it tied to his car and he was driving along the river bank parallel to us. He had picked a spot where a dirt road ran along the river for several miles.

By the time he began to reel us in, we were ready for dry land. But I will never forget the confidence I got from that adventure and the lesson that you can give your kids a lot of fun and still have a long rope to keep them from drowning.

Going Free Range

Free-Range Baby Step: Next birthday, get your child a toy that doesn't require batteries. (Then run.)

Free-Range Brave Step: Send your kids out with their friends and promise to let them teach you whatever game they make up. Accept that this may well involve some minor humiliation.

Giant Leap for Free-Range Kind: This is an idea I got from Richard Louv's *Last Child in the Woods*, a beautiful plea for more nature time for kids. Since one reason kids are not outside is that parents are afraid of what might happen to them, Louv suggests contacting the neighbors and organizing what he calls a "play watch group." Everyone takes turns sitting on the stoop a couple hours each week, being the eyes of the neighborhood. Yes, this does involve some community organizing. But lately we've seen how far community organizers can go.

Commandment 14

Listen to Your Kids

They Don't Want to Be Treated Like Babies (Except the Actual Babies, of Course)

How do you bake an Independence Cake?

A construction-paper poster in a sixth-grade classroom explains the steps. The poster is enormous, because the girl who made it decided that such a cake involves a whole lot of things. Walking to the grocery—alone. Shopping for the ingredients—alone. Walking home—alone. Etc., etc. When the cake is finally baking, it fills the air with something sweeter than devil's food. Can you smell it?

Independence.

Natalie Kolba went through all that for extra credit in her social studies class at a New York City school called, bizarrely enough, NEST + m. (That's New Explorations into Science, Technology & Math, in case you were wondering.) The class is taught by twenty-something Joanna Drusin, who had read about Izzy's solo subway ride and had her students read about it too. When they were done, she told them: OK, now it's your turn. Go do something Free Range.

The eleven-year-olds jumped into action and tried everything from making dinner to running errands to walking to school—all the kinds of sweet, simple things they would have been doing without a second thought if they'd been born in 1957 instead of 1997.

What was different was their heightened sense of adventure—and trepidation: "I thought they were going to abduct me," wrote a young man who took the subway by himself to Saturday morning soccer practice. A girl who made a sunny-side-up egg all by herself admitted, "I was scared out of my wits that I was going to burn the apartment down." Another boy proudly walked the five blocks to and from his local grocery, only to learn that his mom had been trailing him the whole time. Though he lives in one of New York's safest, fanciest neighborhoods, he understood her impulse: "She was just worried." Yet despite these fears on everyone's part, the kids all loved their projects.

"I made it to the field with a grin on my face," said Nikhil Massand. He's the one who was afraid he was going to be abducted.

I visited Drusin's classroom the day the students—five classes' worth—handed in their assignments. Dozens of essays, posters, and mini-books festooned the room, describing Free-Range adventures with a lot of photos and exclamation points. One girl, Emma Evans, wrote up her visit to the vet as a TV news report:

Reporter 1: "Our top story of the day is about a young girl who thought taking her dog to the vet by herself would be one of the big responsibilities of having a dog. Her parents believed the same. Then came the big day and when she went to the vet she was ignored, harassed and humiliated! Charlotte is live there at the scene. It's all yours, Charlotte."

Charlotte: "All right, if you remember we were in the middle of our live broadcast about a young girl at the vet's."

The shot goes live to an examining room, where the door opens to reveal, at last, the lady veterinarian. And at this point Emma abandons TV script form and switches into traditional story mode, like so:

"The vet searched the room for someone, ignoring Emma almost like she was not there. 'Good morning,' Emma said and the vet turned sharply around.

"'Hi. Where is your mommy, little girl?' Her sharp voice echoed against the green walls. A little surprised by the vet's tone, Emma answered that her mom was at work. The vet looked troubled. 'Do you have your mom's phone number with you? I might have to give her a call.' She quickly dialed the given number. 'Hi! This is Dr. S. Your daughter is here. Can I actually give her instructions?'"

In the end, the vet wrote a page of doggie dos and don'ts and handed it to Emma. "Oh wait!" The vet snatched the letter back. "Can you read?"

It's a kids-are-considered-dumb-as-dirt world out there, as Emma and some of the other students learned. But that's part of what happens when you barrel into the adult world head-on.

"Why do you think we did this?" Ms. Drusin asked her class. "Have I just gone completely crazy? Why did we do this?"

Hands shot up in the air. (NEST is a school you have to test to get into. These kids are achievers.) The teacher pointed to a young man. "Yes?"

"Well, our lives aren't that exciting. Maybe we have a few after-school hobbies, but mostly we go home and do our homework. You wanted us to do something exciting."

Another hand went up. "You wanted us to see what we could achieve—do something that might be a little scary at first."

"The whole idea was to see we don't always need help doing something," said another student.

And all of those were absolutely right. (More prosaic but also absolutely right was the boy who said, "To get better grades?")

But it was more than all that, too. As Drusin explained to her students, the school's theme this year is *exploration*—a word you don't hear much in childhood anymore, except when it's, "Let's explore why you think the colonists rebelled." The explorations are all intellectual. But because sixth grade is the first year of middle school, Drusin felt it was time for her kids to try the other kind of exploring. The kind that got the colonists to America in the first place. And if you're wondering how it felt for some of the other kids to do it, read on.

"For the very first time in my life, I decided to go shopping by myself to make a cake to surprise my parents," begins the Independence Cake baker, Natalie. But "without my mom next to me, being further than three blocks from my house, I started to feel strange. I even jumped when some older woman asked me, 'Where is your mommy, young lady?'" The store was half a mile from Natalie's home, and on the way, she says, "I saw all these people and they looked angry to me—like everyone was about to reach out and snatch me." This first solo walk of hers was "no laughing matter at all."

Neither, as it turns out, was paying for the ingredients: "Spending your own allowance is not easy!" (Tell me about it.) But she did it anyway, to make sure the cake was truly, even financially, independent. Then she gathered her bags, started home, and discovered something startling: "The way back home seemed much shorter and more pleasant. Everything bad just flew away because I was already used to the walk."

That same experience—terror on the way to a place and euphoria on the way back—echoed through several of the kids' stories. Over and over they were shocked and delighted to find themselves more capable than they had ever imagined. It's like one of those dreams: suddenly, you're flying.

The other dreamlike part of the adventure was how everything familiar became a little less familiar once the kids were on their own.

"I knew where I was going," wrote Megan Mullaney of her walk to a grocery store. "But it was sort of like a different experience. Even though you've been there before, you're more aware of your surroundings."

We forget that one of the great joys of childhood is exactly that feeling: how the world that you drifted through holding on to your mother's hand becomes *your* world when you start to navigate it on your own. And that's as true of experiences as it is of landscapes. A girl who cooked all her own meals for a day declared, "Even though I knew what I had achieved was not that special, it still *felt* special." Of course it did. Like a first kiss or first car, a whole new part of life had just begun.

Though most of the parents had not expected it this soon, a whole new part of life was beginning for them, too. The part where you start to let go.

This was not easy for all of them. One mom was not going to let her daughter do the project she proposed—knocking on neighbors' doors in their apartment building to say hello—until the daughter came up with a compelling argument: "But mom, if there's ever a fire, they could help us!"

Her door knocking netted her two new friends the same age who go to a different school. "And now we say hi to these people all around us."

So what happens to the kids with parents—and there were several in Ms. Drusin's class—who forbid them to try any kind of independent adventure? Well, I'm pretty sure most of them will end up just fine. Just because parents won't let their eleven-year-old walk the dog doesn't mean they won't let their fifteen-year-old start taking driving lessons or their seventeen-year-old leave for college. And also, just because people complain about their overprotective parents doesn't mean that they wouldn't find something else to complain about if their parents had let them join the circus at age eight and unicycle up the interstate to get there. That being said, there is nonetheless a lot of resentment out there among grown children who feel that their parents instilled in them *too much fear.*

"I'm twenty-six years old and grew up with an extremely overprotective parent who convinced me (unintentionally, unknowingly) that eventually I would be abducted by someone and, most likely, killed," begins a fairly typical letter to the Free-Range Kids Web site. "It took me YEARS (and therapy) to overcome the fear she unintentionally instilled in me. I am still afraid of the dark, of dogs, of strange men. I live in a gated community and I am always looking over my shoulder."

Another Free-Range visitor recalls the abrupt end to her freedom. "I was a Free-Range kid up until nine years old," she wrote. After school she'd spend an hour or so each day just walking around her small town, thinking about things, singing to herself, and enjoying the fact that she wasn't home with her four siblings. But in 1998, all that changed—a fact she blames on ratcheted-up abduction mania on TV.

Suddenly, "to my dismay, my young mom (who was only trying to be a 'good' parent) told me that I was not allowed to take walks by myself anymore, because someone 'can just come and take you.' Why did my parent start to think this way, even though she knew before that I'd always been safe? Why did she suddenly decide that other people could not be trusted to detect anything suspicious involving a child and an adult in the middle of the day, on the sidewalk? It's because the TV news is louder than the truth you see outside."

Most of the children of very fearful parents seemed to understand—at least in adulthood—that their parents were protecting them only out of love. But still, resentment brewed: "There are so many things I don't know how to do because they were so protective of me." "To this day I rue not being less afraid." "I always wished I was pushed more to do things on my own." Those are just a few of the many Free-Range posts by people who'd longed for their parents to show more faith in them.

"My grade school was half a mile away; I was NEVER allowed to walk there or back," wrote another. "My high school was a city bus ride away, but I was never allowed to ride it, and I was not allowed to drive. I asked [my mom] if it was because she didn't trust me." The mom replied: Of course not! She just didn't trust every-one *else*.

As it turns out, that is an extremely common thing for parents to say, and most likely they even believe it. But because the end result is exactly the same—no freedom, constant surveillance—the children end up feeling belittled and distrusted. Ever been in love with someone who takes you out for coffee, then drops the bomb: "It's not you, it's me"? Of course you have. Ever believe it? Of course you didn't. Kids don't believe it either. When parents don't trust them to cross the street or go where they say they're going or buy groceries by themselves because "everyone else" out there is so untrustworthy, kids hear the simultaneous translation: we don't trust *you*.

Parents, teachers, relatives, mentors—the grown-ups in our lives who *do* believe in us have an impact beyond measure. There's a Dr. Phil exercise where he asks you to write down the five people who have had the most effect on your life, good or bad. If you do this (call me a lightweight—I did, and it was utterly illuminating), you will probably find that all the shining stars are the people who believed in you.

I still thank Mrs. MacDougall, a salty, grey-haired seventh-grade social studies teacher who tapped me to accompany her on a trip to southern Illinois in the late seventies. She wanted to go check out a decrepit one-room schoolhouse she was thinking of buying. Her idea was to restore it and take her suburban Chicago students down there for a week every year to *really* feel what life was like in the olden days. She was going to make them use an outhouse and write on slates. Their history books would stop at the Civil War. Cool, right? I'd been her teacher's pet in junior high and stayed very much in touch, so she called to ask me to share the four-hour drive, and we'd stay overnight in the small town's hotel.

"But Ms. Mac, I have school," I told her.

She said this would be educational.

"But Ms. Mac, I'm not sure my mom will let me."

Mom did.

"Ms. Mac," I finally broke it to her. "I don't have a license."

"Do you have your learner's permit?"

"Yes."

"Then let's go!"

That's why this book is dedicated to her.

The people who show us they believe in us are the wind beneath our wings. The black holes are the people who don't. If you think back on the big turning points in your life, good and bad, you will find all those people standing there, directing traffic.

At some point, the ones who believe in us trust us to cross the street. And to drive with just a learner's permit.

REAL WORLD

Every Time I See a Kid with a Sucker or a Scarf, My Sympathetic Nervous System Goes Crazy

A Free-Range visitor writes:

> At 20, I am part of the generation that has grown up with "helicopter" parents. Although I am grateful to my parents for the amount of care and attention they gave me, I definitely feel they went too far in attempting to assure my safety by instilling fear.
>
> I was not allowed to venture out alone pretty much at all until my teens, and even now, warnings from my mother ring in my ears when crossing a busy street or heading out at night. Although this has encouraged me to make safe choices, every time I see a kid with a sucker or a scarf, my sympathetic nervous system goes crazy as I am sure a tragedy is about to occur.
>
> I think it must be hard to find an appropriate balance as to how much freedom to give a child, but based on my own level of paranoia, I would tend to think that more freedom is beneficial as long as it is given with the appropriate information and safety reminders.

Going Free Range

Free-Range Baby Step: Even grade-school children can come up with a Free-Range project that will make them feel more independent, such as learning how to fry an egg or fetching you something from the neighbors. Or baking an Independence Cake!

Free-Range Brave Step: This one guarantees that you will change along with your child. Have your middle schooler start doing a task that *you* would normally do, like taking the dog to the vet or buying the groceries for dinner. Once your children are old enough to drive, have them take Grandma to the doctor or return things to the store. You'll be a little more free, and so will they.

Giant Leap for Free-Range Kind: Mrs. MacDougall took junior high students on two-week archeological digs in the blistering-hot soybean fields of southern Illinois. This was the kind of thing only done by college students back then—the seventies—but Ms. Mac believed that tweens were just as capable of digging and sifting and sweltering and living in an abandoned house-turned-dorm as anyone else. Once we junior diggers got back home to suburbia, she had us give slide shows to civics groups. She invited us to dinner at her Victorian home, in twos or threes, and even to her grown-up Christmas party, teeming with journalists (which is, I think, why I became one). All of which is a long way of saying that mentors can change a child's life as surely as any parent. If you want to take a giant leap for Free-Range Kind, look out for some kids you relate to and bring them into your circle. Give them opportunities to work with you, or for you, and have them be a part of some grown-up experiences. Most adults remember someone besides their parents who played a great role in their youth. That person can be you.

Part 2

The Free-Range Guide to Life

Safe or Not?

The A-to-Z Review of Everything You Might Be Worried About

R eader advisory: in truth, this section might not address your *every* worry because you probably have some worries I've never even thought of. For instance, if you have moved to a neighborhood plagued by deadly spiders, all I can say is:

Deadly spiders? My god. Deadly? Spiders? *Deadly spiders?*

Which may not be a whole lot of help.

Likewise, if you are worried about a huge issue like global warming and how it will affect your child, I don't get into that here either, even though I'm sure its long-term effects are a lot scarier than whatever might happen if your kid takes a swig of Children's NyQuil before age four. (See "Cough and Cold Medicinitis," below.) Giant, societal issues are not ones that you can choose or not choose for your children. Whether or not to give them kiddie cough medicine is.

So maybe "everything you might be worried about" is a bit too broad. Still, I hope this section will prove a handy reference many of the times you hear about something else to add to your Worry List, and wonder if you really have to. Here's what this reporter-skeptic-worrier-mom found out about fears from A to Z, starting with . . .

Animals, Being Eaten By

This is a prospect no parent likes to contemplate. Even nonparents don't like to contemplate it. In fact, it's hard to find anyone who really likes to contemplate the idea of someone they love being eaten by a wild animal. Fortunately, you really don't have to.

Although a tiger did escape its cage at the San Francisco Zoo in 2007, killing one young man and mauling two others, this kind of thing is so rare that you have to go back to Siegfried and Roy's fateful Vegas performance of October 3, 2003, for another instance of severe, all-body mauling. That night, Roy was bitten in the neck and dragged off stage by his ferocious costar. (The tiger one.) Amazingly, he survived.

The few other instances of ferocious animals attacking humans usually occurred when those humans worked at the zoo and forgot to properly close a cage door or two. Teach your children to pay attention to details, and doors, and even if they grow up to be zookeepers, they should be fine.

Bats (Metal)

Are metal bats more dangerous than wooden ones, if and when a kid actually manages to hit the ball?

Little League issued a statement in 2007 that basically boiled down to this: further research must be done. The fact that they haven't thrown metal bats into the recycling heap means, to me, that they aren't exceedingly worried about them. So neither am I.

No matter what bat you're using, baseball is a pretty safe game. The largest study of high school baseball injuries to date found that baseball had lower injury rates than other high school sports. (And need I remind a certain young reader: that is why some mothers insist on *flag* football no matter how "cool" it would be to wear padding.)

Metal bats do seem to make it easier for players to hit the ball a little harder and faster, which in turn may make it tougher for youngsters to catch that ball (or to duck). But still, the chances of being killed by any ball hit by any young person turn out to be three million to one. It is hard to lower a number like that without replacing the bats with paper towel tubes. (Something I'd be willing to do. But I'm not a big sports fan.)

Simply banning metal bats may not make a difference at all. The best study of metal versus wood was conducted in 2007 by researchers at the Illinois State University's School of Kinesiology and Recreation. In five conferences, players were instructed to use wood bats in conference play and metal bats in nonconference games. After more than five hundred games and twenty thousand at-bats involving about fifty teams, the researchers found "no statistically significant evidence that non-wood bats result in an increased incidence or severity of injury."

It's hard to believe anything as ugly as a metal bat is as safe as a beautiful wooden one, but that seems to be the case. In any event, paper towel tubes are still an option.

Bats (Vampire)

Avoid these.

Bottle Feeding: Formula for Disaster?

I try not to bear grudges, but this is one I do. Hey, it's only been thirteen years. I was out with my firstborn son; he was about three months old, and he was crying. A vague acquaintance of mine inquired, "Oh, are you breastfeeding him?"

Of course it was none of her business, but stupidly I answered her. "Yes."

"*Exclusively* breastfeeding him?"

"No. Sometimes I give him a bottle in the middle of the night."

"A-*ha!*" she said. "That's why he's crying."

That kind of conversation is why this is such a difficult issue to discuss. There are many breastfeeding advocates who believe that bottle feeding is tantamount to child abuse—something only a negligent, selfish, or at least clueless mother would do to her baby.

But the U.S. Department of Health and Human Services reports that 87 percent of mothers are not exclusively breastfeeding by six months. So if you are bottle feeding, you are hardly alone. Is it possible that 87 percent of all moms are bad? Please. Formula is not rat poison. It's something that millions and millions of babies have grown up on, even from their first sip (including me). Is it every bit as perfect as breast milk?

Maybe not. But there will be a thousand child-rearing decisions you will make before your baby leaves for that gap year in Kenya: Organic Oreos? Speech therapy for the minor lisp? Private driving lessons? And there is no way every single one will be optimal. It's hard to believe when you're brand new at parenting, but breastfeeding is just one of those many decisions, and, like all the rest, it is not the be-all and end-all that will determine your baby's health and happiness. (Even though busybodies may tell you it is. Walk away, fast, or you'll end up with a twelve-year grudge.)

There *is* evidence that breastfeeding provides some advantages to a baby, but not big ones you'd be able to spot a mile away. Chiefly it seems to cut down on ear infections (by 19 percent), recurrent ear infections (80 percent), and diarrhea (50 percent). These are usually not illnesses with long-term effects. Some studies also suggest that breastfed babies may have slightly higher IQs, but who knows if that's because they were breastfed or because breastfeeding moms may have higher IQs or because breastfed kids grow up in houses filled with books (on breastfeeding)? And are you trying to raise a genius or trying to raise a child and doing it as best you can? As Rebecca Kukla says, our obsession with long-term breastfeeding "seems to be much more about our image of appropriate motherhood than the nutritional well-being of infants." And she's a professor of obstetrics, gynecology, and philosophy. She thinks hard about healthy babies!

As for bonding and such, Kukla points to a 2008 study, reported in the journal *Pediatrics*—the largest study ever to assess the long-term effects of breastfeeding on child behavior—that found no difference in baby-mommy bonding whether moms breastfed exclusively or not. The study followed a whopping fourteen thousand mom-kid pairs for six-and-a-half years, and the researchers frankly admitted that if nothing else, they had expected to find "behavioral advantages conferred by more exclusive or prolonged breastfeeding." But they didn't. Whether breastfed for a long time or not, given lots of bottles or none, the tykes were interchangeable.

Meantime, a recent study of infants and toddlers at Children's Hospital in Boston found that the breastfed ones were up to ten times more likely to be deficient in vitamin D, a condition that can lead to the bone-softening disease rickets, because they were not getting the extra vitamin D that's added to formula. I write this not to terrify any breastfeeders but just to point out that once again, there's no absolutely "right" way to raise a child.

Two of my close friends could not breastfeed, and it was not for lack of trying. They called in lactation consultants. They sat for hours with aquarium-sized mechanical pumps, trying to squeeze out more than a drop or two from the breasts they resented like hell. They felt like failures when, actually, they were great moms. They didn't let their kids starve. They swallowed their disappointment and went and got formula and gave it to their babies who are now just fine young women, virtually indistinguishable from their bosom-fed buddies.

A lot of moms tend to think that if they don't do everything that natural way—natural childbirth, natural baby feeding, natural whatever—they are less than perfect, and their kids will be too.

But guess what? There's no such thing as perfection, and aiming for it will only drive you crazy. So breastfeed if you can and if you want to. But please don't beat yourself up if you don't. And don't let anyone else beat you up, either.

BPA Poisoning in Baby Bottles, Sippy Cups . . . and Everything Else

Bisphenol A, otherwise known as BPA, is a chemical used to harden plastic. It's in everything from bike helmets to canned food liners to the real bone of contention: baby bottles. In fact, it's been used in baby bottles for the past twenty-five years. The question is, is it dangerous for your kid? And are you a reckless, life-threatening parent if you allow your baby any contact with BPA whatsoever?

In 2008, the Canadian government banned BPA from baby bottles, calling it "toxic." The health department there believes BPA could have some neural effects on young children and pregnant women, and declared its official stance, "Better safe than sorry." Stores including Wal-Mart and Toys "R" Us announced plans to phase out BPA in children's products, too.

At the same time, however, the U.S. Food and Drug Administration declared that at the levels we are exposed to BPA in normal, everyday life, it's safe, even for children. And although the agency continues to study this chemical, its findings were right in step with Europe and Japan, both of whose health ministries found BPA safe, as did the Harvard Center for Risk Analysis.

The worry is that BPA sometimes, when administered to rodents, seems to disrupt their hormones. But what the folks at Harvard found is that these claims "have generally been based on small-scale studies, using non-validated protocols, and the results have not been independently replicated." Nor were the adverse results "found in much larger-scale multigenerational studies." In other words, the studies just did not hold up scientifically, in the opinion of this Harvard panel. The panel was chaired by the former medical director of the March of Dimes—the nonprofit organization dedicated to eradicating birth defects. It's unlikely that he would give a pass to any chemical he truly found worrisome.

Another heavyweight who believes BPA is safe is Calvin Willhite, a toxicologist at the California Department of Toxic Substances Control. Yes, California, a state not known to take its toxic threats lightly. Willhite points out that "many of the studies that show adverse effects in rodents given small doses of bisphenol A used subcutaneous injections." That is, the rats or mice were given shots of the chemical. But babies aren't shooting up BPA. They're exposed to it when they drink from plastic cups and bottles. Turns out that when the rats and mice were exposed to it that way, too—orally—most studies "did not show adverse effects, even at high doses."

Remember, too, that if you don't heat your bottles, there is even less chance of anything leaching. So if you love plastic containers but are still a little leery, you can give your kids unheated drinks. There's no law that says they have to drink their milk warm.

Dr. F. Sessions Cole, who, among other things, is head of newborn medicine at the St. Louis Children's Hospital, understands the fears. "We've actually looked at this pretty carefully, because [BPA] is in all of the tubing in the neonatal intensive care unit. We're running a lot of liquid through this tubing into a lot of very sick babies, and if the concern is raised to a sufficiently high level, we'd be among the first to stop using it. I don't want to make babies unsafe! On the other hand, I don't want to throw away strategies and equipment that are working fine. I have a lot of babies doing great, getting medicine through BPA tubes."

If very sick preemies are not being adversely affected by BPA, it's hard to imagine anyone else is. But of course, this is yet another one of those parenting decisions that's up to you. If you'd feel better using glass bottles, there's no reason not to. There just doesn't seem to be a clear and compelling reason not to use the plastic ones either, if that's what you prefer.

Cell Phones and Brain Cancer (but Not, Alas, "Cell Phones and How Come Your Kids Never Answer When You Need Them To")

Is there a connection between brain tumors and cell phones?

Not according to Nirit Weiss—and she's a brain surgeon. "The vast majority of studies show absolutely no correlation," says the specialist at Mt. Sinai Hospital in New York. "National studies, European studies—nothing has pointed to either malignant or benign brain tumors."

Still, some people remain terrified, so Weiss went on to explain, "Brain tumors in my world are very common, but in the real world, they are very uncommon." When patients come in for surgery and wonder if they caused their own cancer by too much chatting, "I always say forget it. There's absolutely nothing related to it at all." (Then the patients say, "Sorry—what were you just saying? I was listening to my messages.")

In the book *Future Files*, Richard Watson points out that humans greet most new technologies with fear, just as we're doing today. "The invention of the telegraph created a widespread belief that signals would interfere with the weather, while the introduction of trains and automobiles was predicted to create a variety of physical and mental disorders." When electric street lights first replaced gas lamps, people feared them the way we fear cell phone towers today.

And the phones themselves.

Neurosurgeon Weiss says that while the studies she cites have been done on adults, not kids, she believes that the safety benefits of a child carrying a phone "far outweigh any known risks associated with cell phones."

Whether the benefits of having your kid spend all day texting her friends outweigh any other risks—that's up to you.

Choking on Food and All the Other Little Things Around the House

"Keep Kids Safe!" screams the warning on the box of Fruit Gushers candy. "To avoid choking, give Fruit Flavored Snacks only to children who can easily swallow chewy foods. Children should be seated and supervised while eating."

Because, of course, candy eating is right up there with knife throwing—or so the warnings make it seem. But what kind of threat does choking really pose?

The statistics, as collected by the U.S. Consumer Product Safety Commission (CPSC), show that in 2000, 160 children under the age of fourteen died from inhaling or ingesting something that choked them. About half the time that something was food; the other half of the time it was an object, like a coin.

The children *most* likely to choke on food are under age four and especially under age one—simply because the very young don't have a lot of teeth. So the CPSC and just about every other body that concerns itself with child safety recommend that you avoid feeding your young kids round, firm foods, such as grapes and hot-dogs and carrots. If you *do* feed your kids these foods, they suggest you cut them into pea-size pieces.

The food, that is.

This seems like fine advice, but it's not something I did consistently, nor do most parents. When you're at the zoo and you get your over-one-year-old a hot dog, the odds that he will die from choking at that very moment—or any moment that year—are about 1 in 350,000. Small.

Still, it certainly makes sense to try to keep the kid areas in your home as free as possible of small objects such as buttons, change, hearing aid batteries, marbles, and even balloons, since kids (and if you happen to live underwater, fish and turtles) can accidentally suck these in.

Foods to watch out for? The aforementioned hard, round ones, as well as nuts, seeds, hard candy, and chunks of cheese. Avoid chunks of meat, too, because those can be hard even for us experienced eaters to chew successfully.

Your kids will have plenty of time for tough meat when they get to college.

And by the way, remember how you were never supposed to hit anyone on the back if he was choking because it would only make things worse? Well it's back to making things better. The American Red Cross now recommends leaning the choker over and giving five sharp blows to the back, followed by five abdominal thrusts—ye olde Heimlich maneuver—from the front. And don't forget to call 911 if these aren't doing the trick. (With any luck, you have not thrown out your phone for fear of it causing brain cancer.)

Cough and Cold Medicinitis

Parents spend $2 billion a year on over-the-counter cough and cold medicine for their kids—and that's not counting all the Lipton chicken noodle soup. Is it dangerous?

Well, for sure not the soup (unless we start that whole discussion about too much salt in the diet, but let's not. I love salt). As for the drugs, the Food and Drug Administration does not recommend using any of the over-the-counter cough and cold meds on children under age two. Recently fearing that the FDA might bump that age up to six, most drug manufacturers voluntarily changed their labeling to say that their cough and cold meds are no longer meant for children under age four.

Above that age? It's up to you. The chance that your child will die from these meds is microscopically small. In 2004–2005, there were three cases of infant death due to ingesting cough and cold remedies. But those were infants, who aren't supposed to take that medicine anymore. And of course, you should never give your kids any of the adult meds you have lying around, be they over-the-counter or prescription. And keep them all out of reach, etc., etc., even though most adults can barely get them open, much less a toddler. (Blister packs are the worst, agreed? I have actually forgone some medication because I couldn't peel back the paper and puncture the Kryptonite bubble.)

Anyway, the *real* reason to be skeptical about over-the-counter kiddie cold remedies is that "bottom line, they don't really work." So says my own pediatrician, Harris Burstin, who teaches pediatrics at New York University. Once in a while he will recommend an antihistamine, like Benadryl. But mostly he recommends using a humidifier or vaporizer, or even steaming up the bathroom for sniffly kids.

And I personally recommend salty, yummy chicken soup.

Death by Stroller

If you go on the Consumer Product Safety Commission's Web site, you will find an alert reminding parents, "Infants Can Die When Their Heads Become Trapped in Strollers."

Which is true. Infants can die when their heads become trapped in anything, and it's an awful thing to contemplate. But how *many* children under age five die when their heads become trapped in strollers? The answer is . . . one to two a year.

If we worry about every incident that can harm one or two children out of about twenty million kids under age five, there is no way we can possibly let them do anything at all. Eat? They could choke. Sleep? There's SIDS. Crawl? They could die from a concussion. Take a bath? They could drown. Just sit there not doing anything (but not in a stroller)? Sounds like a plan!

In Australia just a few years back, two infants died when the strollers they were in rolled away from their caregivers and down into a river. This led to a huge outcry, against not the river gods but lax stroller standards. From now on, all strollers should come equipped with wrist straps, the public demanded. Strollers should not budge unless an adult is actively squeezing the handle to unlock the brake. A spokeswoman for a group called Standards Australia announced, "If any good can come of this tragedy, it is that better standards will be introduced."

But when it comes to stroller safety, standards are extremely high already. In the United States, for example, a company called Regal Lager recalled its "e3" buggies in 2006 because it learned that children could touch the rear tires when in the stroller's add-on seat, creating an "abrasion hazard." The company had received one report of a child who had scraped his arm this way. One report! Of a scrape! Another company recalled twenty-five thousand of its "Ranger" strollers after it received thirty-nine reports of a lock mechanism breaking, with one report of a baby's arm being pinched.

We are so convinced that we can make the world 101 percent safe that the idea of a child suffering even a pinch or scrape seems mercilessly, litigiously cruel. And I guess we have to thank the litigiously minded folks who came before us and created such a safe, accountable world of baby products. But the other legacy of that litigation is our now impossible-to-assuage fear that any product can and may well kill our kids.

Too bad they don't sell pacifiers for adults. We need something to calm us down. (Then again, they're probably a choking hazard. Or addictive. Or toxic.)

Eating Snow

Go ahead and eat it. It's the other other white meat.

Despite headlines like "White Stuff Is Full of Bacteria" and "Snow Eating Now Endangered Kid Pleasure" and "Study Warns Against Snow," it turns out that the study that caused this media flurry (sorry) did *not* warn against eating snow.

But it should have warned against slow news days.

What happened was that in 2008, an article in the magazine *Science* reported that when snow forms, it clings to little particles and—this was the big news—sometimes those particles happen to be the bacteria that cause disease in some plants, including tomatoes and green beans.

So if your child is a tomato or green bean, *steer clear*. Otherwise? Don't worry. As Joel Forman, a member of the American Academy of Pediatrics committee on environmental health, was quoted as saying, "I can say that I'm not aware of any clinical reports of children becoming ill from eating snow. And I looked."

It does not matter to our health how snow forms. What matters—and always has—is whether it's yellow.

Germs, Antigerms, and Shopping Cart Liners

If only Howard Hughes had been born in our day, he might have been seen as a perfectly normal guy, instead of as a bizarre, billionaire germophobe.

Well, he'd still be a billionaire (unless he invested in Lehman Brothers, Fannie Mae, Bear Sterns, real estate, CitiBank, or newspapers). But at least he could carry around a pump of hand sanitizing gel and no one would find it loopy. He could swab every surface in sight with antibacterial towelettes. He could bring his own disposable placemats to restaurants (albeit covered with characters like Dora the Explorer) and his own disposable kiddie gloves (covered with penguins). They really do sell those gloves now, so kids don't have to touch anything. They're called "gLovies," but I'd call them "OCD Training Mitts."

Anyway, once Howard got to the supermarket, he could plop his mittened moppets into a shopping cart liner—a cloth basket you bring with you that fits into the part of the cart you normally put a kid in, with little holes for the legs. That way no part of the child need ever come in contact with what some parents apparently consider a leper colony on wheels: the cart they may well have already disinfected with the free wipes many groceries now provide at the entrance. All of which begs two questions:

Is it really necessary to take any of these antigerm precautions? And could any of them actually backfire and end up doing more harm than good?

First things first, says Dr. William Schaffner, chairman of the Department of Preventive Medicine at Vanderbilt and a member of the Infectious Diseases Society of America (which sounds like a society where Mad Cow Disease and TB go to kick back and swap war stories, but is actually an association of about eight thousand members who study disease and how it is spread).

To the question of whether or not one should carry around hand sanitizing gels or antibacterial wipes, Schaffner replied, "It's like, 'Did you buy the blue Ford or the red Chevy?' It's really a matter of choice." Parents who exhibit what he calls "hygienic exuberance" may feel reassured using the wipes and gels, and these products generally do go to work on the germs kids are so intent upon picking up and disseminating. But so do soap and water, for the most part. On the other hand (I guess the dirty one), we live in a microbial world, and all of us are covered with microbes. "That is the human condition," says Schaffner, not something new and awful to suddenly get worked up about.

In any event, far more important than wiping our kids clean, he says, is this: make sure they get vaccinated against infectious diseases.

Now, as for whether we are becoming too clean for our own good, that is a still a matter of debate.

The debate began in 1989 with a report by David Strachan, a researcher who had been studying a sample of 17,414 British children all born during one week in 1958. One of the things Strachan noticed was that the younger children in bigger families were less likely than the other kids to develop eczema and allergies like hay fever. He speculated that maybe this was because their older siblings brought home so many infections that this somehow gave the younger brothers and sisters immunity against some illnesses.

What's more, as hygiene has improved over the last fifty years and family size has shrunk, kids are getting less exposed to infections when they're younger, and that may be why we are seeing rising rates of things like asthma and allergies. Strachan's conjecture is now known as the "hygiene hypothesis," and it dovetails with the fascinating fact that children in less-developed, frankly dirtier countries have less asthma.

Other scientists intrigued by this idea developed other experiments whose results seemed to suggest the same thing: the more exposure an immune system gets when it's very young, the stronger it seems to grow. A 1999 study in Wisconsin comparing rural kids who grew up on farms to rural kids who did not grow up on farms found that the farm kids—especially the ones exposed to cattle—had 50 percent less asthma. Another study found that infants six to twelve months old who go to day care are 75 percent less likely to develop asthma than their stay-at-home counterparts.

So does that mean, to keep our children safe, we should slather them in dung and pack them off to Tiny Tot Town?

Uh. Maybe not just yet. But do we need to slather them in Purell and perch them in shopping carts liners? That's probably not necessary either. But as Dr. Schaffner reminds us: vaccinations are.

Halloween Candy: Hershey's Kiss of Death?

If you want to read all about how Halloween has become a fearmonger's dream, since it's the perfect storm of parents, children, independence, food, and would-be fun, go read Commandment 7.

(And why, may I ask, did you not read this book in traditional front-to-back fashion? Just please don't tell me you've skipped other chapters, too!) But if you just want to know if it's safe to let your kids eat their candy before you inspect it—before you even lay eyes (or hands or teeth) on it—the answer is yes.

Let them eat all those slightly ragged Reese's packs and even that shiny red apple. (As if they'd ever eat an apple when they've got a bag of candy in front of them.) There has never been a single substantiated instance of any child dying from a stranger's poisoned Halloween candy.

But there are some other very scary trends I can substantiate for you.

Some American towns are moving Halloween to the Sunday before October 31 so kids can trick-or-treat during the afternoon, and afternoon only. So much for a centuries-old nighttime holiday.

A growing "Green Halloween" movement in Seattle is campaigning against any sweets that are not 100 percent straight from the hive. Normal candy bars would be verboten.

And in California (where else?), a woman who didn't want her children to be scared by a nearby lawn covered with tombstones and scary-looking monsters called the local police to report a "hate crime."

Who, precisely, does she believe the lawn decorator hates? Children? Moms? The protoplasmically challenged?

Unclear. But eating Halloween candy? All clear.

Internet Predators and Other Skeeves Online

Maybe you've seen that big ad campaign that says one in seven youths will receive a sexual solicitation over the Internet. So should you pull your PC's plug right now?

No. Especially considering that one of the researchers who came up with that statistic, David Finkelhor, says the problem is not that simple or—thank goodness—that bad.

Finkelhor is a professor at the University of New Hampshire and founder of the Crimes Against Children Research Center. In an effort to figure out whether the Internet is making life more dangerous for kids, he and his colleagues conducted two studies of about three thousand youths, ages ten to seventeen, to find out if they had been harassed or solicited for sex online.

The one-in-seven statistic turns out to be referring to young people, mostly teens, who received "an unwanted kind of sexual remark or comment or overture online," says Finkelhor. These were not necessarily propositions or even anything explicit. Most, he says, "were the Internet equivalent of wolf whistles."

That includes annoying but basically nonthreatening questions like "What's your bra size?" and "Are you a virgin?" Two-thirds of the youths who received these comments reported that they were not upset by them, and almost all of them handled the solicitations "easily and effectively," according to the study. They did this by either ignoring the question, telling the sender off, blocking the sender (I wish I knew how to do that!), or simply leaving the site.

Moreover, the two studies suggested that the kids who end up attracting more of these remarks and getting into more serious trouble are not simply random young folks who have taken out a MySpace account or who go online to chat with their friends. They are kids who are:

- Communicating online with a lot of people they don't know.
- Going to sexually oriented sites.

Finkelhor also believes they are appearing online in a "sexualized persona." They're using sexy names or decorating their network sites with suggestive stuff. They are, in short, the online versions of the offline provocative kids most of us are familiar with. (And if you're not, kindly observe 90 percent of the characters on *Gossip Girl*.)

Predators, meanwhile, turn out to be smart shoppers. They don't just click on random cuties hoping to seduce them. "That would be a bit like trying to get a date by phoning people from the telephone book," Finkelhor says. Instead, they treat the Internet more like the Yellow Pages. And in a sense, the young people they are looking for advertise, by being very sexual.

Whom do they attract? A year-long study by The Internet Safety Technical Task Force—a group created by forty-nine states' attorneys general to look into online predators—found that the people trolling for underage sex are usually not dirty old men, but people of roughly the same age as the people they're soliciting. After all, most of the liaisons born on the Web promise some sort of satisfaction. A sixteen-year-old girl going off to meet her pixilated paramour who said he's eighteen will not be eager to switch her affections to the forty-five-year-old waiting for her with cheese fries at Denny's.

The real Internet danger lies in your child thinking that she has found someone who cares about her, when actually that "caring" person is a scumbag. The child may even continue to "love" the scumbag and not feel exploited at all.

How can you keep your child from falling into the arms of such slime? It all starts at home. And not with Internet filters.

First of all, you should strive for a fairly open relationship with your children, so you can talk to them about online relationships, including the downside to a relationship with a stranger, particularly if the stranger is older (and still addicted to cheese fries). Always remind your kids that they have the right to say no to anything that makes them feel bad or uncomfortable . . . except for sitting there, listening to you.

You also have to talk to them about how they're presenting themselves on the Web. Degrading pictures attract degrading relationships. Worse: those pictures never disappear. A good way to bring this point home is to ask your child, "Would you feel bad if dad/grandma/the local news team saw what you posted?" Squirming is all to the good.

One thing many parents worry about that turns out not to be true is the myth that social networking sites like MySpace and Facebook make children more vulnerable to online predators. They don't. The worst places to hang out online seem to be public chat rooms where anyone can "wander" in and talk about anything. Which they do.

In short, the Web turns out to work pretty much the same as the "real" world, with some sexual soliciting, yes, but mostly just a lot of socializing, some of it dumb, some meaningful. Moreover, the majority of predators are on the prowl for troubled youth who have a tendency to take risks offline too.

On the bright side: at least they know how to type.

Lead Paint, Lead Toys, and Lead Everything from China

Lead really is bad for kids. So bad that one economist hypothesized that the American crime rate has been dropping since the early nineties thanks to the laws restricting lead in gasoline starting in 1975 and nixing lead paint in 1978.

As children grew up with less and less exposure to lead, fewer and fewer of them grew into addled young adults. And because lead tends to cause problems with impulse control (among other awful things), less lead meant better-behaved kids. At least so goes the theory, by a guy named Rick Nevin, who found the same crime drop in other countries when they outlawed lead too.

Anyway, thanks to those antilead laws, the average level of lead in Americans' blood dropped 90 percent from 1976 to 1996. Now fewer than 2 percent of U.S. kids test positive for elevated lead, so unless you're in a deteriorating home or a particularly polluted part of the country, you're pretty far out of the woods. And yet, these days it just doesn't feel like Christmas without a massive recall of lead-painted toys from China.

Those toys really don't pose a very serious problem if all your child does is play with them. But a lot of toddlers do that toddler thing of sticking toys in their mouths, and that *is* a problem (and gross), because they absorb way more lead by sucking on it. So if a toy has been recalled for lead and you have small children at home, just chuck it. You probably have way too many toys anyway. Meantime, China has promised: no more lead paint on toys it's exporting to the United States. We shall see.

Sydney Spiesel, a professor of pediatrics at Yale, says that toys usually aren't the problem anyway. "Almost every case I've seen of high lead has been a result of either remodeling or painting, where someone wanted to do a really good job and scrape down to the old paint," he says.

The curse of watching *This Old House*. Once old paint is flaking off your pre-1978 walls for whatever reason, you should have your child or home tested for lead. If the level is high, you have to have the paint removed or sealed up, probably professionally. Not fun, not cheap, not easy. But you know what they say: "Get the lead out."

Licking the Batter off Beaters While They Are Still Plugged In

I realize this item may not be of keenest interest to that many readers, but it will be of GREAT VALUE to someone who is normally so smart and responsible but who was apparently overcome by an irresistible urge for peanut butter cookie batter and COULD HAVE SLICED HIS TONGUE OFF THE OTHER NIGHT! You know who you are!

Don't do it.

Plastic Bags and Why There Are Warnings All over Them

One of the many joys of watching *Mad Men* is seeing how worried—*not*—the parents were about their kids, at least in this fictional portrayal of the early sixties.

In one episode, a girl of about six or seven twirls into the kitchen and announces she's a fairy or space monster or something. Her costume consists of a dry cleaning bag.

The mother is horrified! "If I find those clean clothes on the floor, young lady, you are in *big* trouble."

Visions of crumpled clothes, not imminent death, dance in her head.

So I looked up the stats on plastic bags. Are they really so bad, or are we just paranoid? Must we really keep them away from our kids?

Yes and no.

Yes, about twenty-five children do die each year, suffocated by bags. Horrible. But according to the Consumer Product Safety Commission, most of these are children under the age of one. They rolled into a bag and couldn't roll out, or a plastic bag of clothes fell on them and they couldn't get out from underneath and suffocated.

These are terrible stories, but they have nothing to do with a six-year-old twirling around in a bag she can yank off whenever she wants. They are really stories of babies suffocated by babyhood—by not being able to crawl away yet, or even lift a head.

So by all means, keep plastic bags away from infants. Keep bags out of cribs, and do not use them as cheap waterproofing sheets (which is what parents used to do, which is how dry cleaning bags got their bad rap). And don't store big plastic bags of stuff where they can fall on your children. In fact, best not to store anything where it can fall on your children, right?

Once your child is capable of movement, however, plastic bags seem to become a lot less worrisome—just one of the many life lessons we can all learn from *Mad Men*. (The other biggie being that men look better in hats.)

Playground Perils

Playgrounds today are *so* safe, they may be missing a lot of the things you used to like about them: merry-go-rounds, tall slides, children having fun. Our local school is not the only one I've heard of that literally prohibits kids from *running* on the playground, at least in certain areas, at certain times. (Last check, children were still allowed to skip with joyful abandon, if they insisted.)

Despite all this funning down, it still makes sense to get kids out to a playground, because being outside and getting exercise beats the infinitesimal dangers they might encounter there. In England, even the head of the Royal Society for the Prevention of Accidents—a guy whose job is pretty self-explanatory—declared, "A skinned knee or a twisted ankle in a challenging and exciting play environment is not only acceptable, it is a positive necessity to educate our children and to prepare them for a complex, dangerous world."

I don't think he's saying that a twisted ankle is positively necessary for each child, but you get his point. Anyhow, what *are* the chances of your child getting seriously hurt on the playground?

Jolly slim! The odds against dying from a playground injury are four million to one. What's more, of those very rare (fourteen a year or so) deaths, most come as a result of injuries on *home* play sets. Public playgrounds, most of them reequipped since the early eighties when safety guidelines were first drawn up, are an excellent place for children. And if you find one where the kids are still allowed to run, so much the better. Break a leg! (Just an expression, folks. Just an expression.)

Pools and Water and Kids and Toilets (Not the Fun Part)

Pools are dangerous, especially the ones at home, simple as that. Drowning is the second leading cause of death for kids (after car accidents), and 75 percent of the pool drownings occur at home.

So?

So don't let your children swim unattended, obviously. Prevent them and any other neighborhood scamps from getting in without your knowing it by putting a secure fence around the pool and making sure the back door leading out to the pool has a safety lock too. In and of themselves, these measures could prevent 50 to 90 percent of childhood drownings, according to Safe Kids Worldwide. And do not depend on water wings to keep your kid afloat! The kind I bought for my kids cost $.99. Garbage! (So why did I buy them? Well, they were cute. And they did work . . . for a while. But I kept my eyes on the kids when they wore them.)

While we're on the cheery subject of drowning, remember never to leave a baby or young child in the bath alone, either, not even if they're in some device like a bath chair. Those are the tub equivalent of water wings. As for whether or not you need a toilet lock: about four kids die in toilets a year. Less than one in a million.

To me, keeping the door closed seems good enough. (With the kids outside of it. Duh.)

Raw Dough's Raw Deal

Countless kids have been warned not to eat raw cookie dough because of the eggs. But in our home, dough is one of the four major food groups. Imagine my delight, then, upon finding a U.S. Department of Agriculture report from 2002 that determined that, indeed, some raw eggs *do* carry salmonella. How many of them?

A whopping 0.003 percent of the sixty-nine billion eggs produced every year.

That's about one egg in every thirty thousand.

Say you're unlucky enough to eat an infected egg raw. What are your chances of recovering *without* going to the doctor? Ninety-four percent. What are your chances of not recovering and, in fact, dying of this diarrhea-producing disease?

Your chances are 0.05 percent.

The Centers for Disease Control report that seventy-nine people died from egg-born salmonella from 1985 to 1998. That's about six people a year—out of three hundred million.

Even though the young, the elderly, and the ill are the folks most vulnerable to this disease, odds of about fifty million to one are ones I'm willing to take. And I let my kids take them too. (But not when the beaters are still plugged in! See above.)

School Shootings

The alarm goes off, the teacher flies to lock the door, and the kids sit rigidly at their desks, awaiting further instructions—or doom.

It's a lockdown drill, the kind used in schools across the country to prepare for a Columbine-type killing or terrorist attack. Are those really something we need to worry about?

No. Not that shootings never occur at schools, but they are so few and far between that kids are actually safer at school than almost anyplace else. Consider that of all the homicides of school-age kids, only 1.4 percent actually take place *at* school. (This does not count the kids who die of boredom.)

Besides, schools are becoming safer and safer. Theft at school is down by more than 50 percent since 1992, and so is violent crime.

Although it's hard to shake the fear of something as graphic as Columbine, educators should get a grip. One school district in Massachusetts has gone so far as to propose training children age ten and up to fight crazed gunmen using their backpacks and text-books. (Stop or I'll give you a pop quiz on early American history!)

This seems more hysterical than helpful, considering that those kids—all kids—have literally a 0.0003 percent chance of being killed at school. Math teachers, please explain: those are very, very long odds.

Spoilage (of Children)

You can't spoil a baby by holding it too much, that much I know. And positive reinforcement beats negative at every age (even ninety). Positive reinforcement isn't spoiling unless a pony is involved more than once.

Beyond that? Here's the simple, brilliant, antispoiling trick a housepainter from Pakistan taught my friend: every week, run out of one thing. Orange juice, cereal—whatever. It's a way to get kids used to not always having exactly what they want exactly when they want it.

Spoilage (of Lunch)

On a field trip a few years back, one of the moms looked anything but jolly. Because the trip was to the park, the kids had been told to bring their lunches in disposable bags. You know—the brown paper kind?

"I just hope it's OK," the mom fretted.

"What's OK?" I asked.

"My daughter's lunch! It's not in an insulated bag. I hope the sandwich doesn't spoil!"

"Did you bring *your* lunch to school in an insulated bag?" I asked. She shook her head. "So why are you worried now?"

She didn't give an answer so allow me to supply one. Back when we were kids they didn't *sell* insulated bags, so no one worried about needing one. But now that some marketing genius has come up with those bags and even, God help us, little ice packs to keep your child's apple slices crisp and cold, the idea of a room temperature tuna sandwich sounds to some like death on toast.

But here's the deal: Your kid's tuna salad is going to be just fine because—surprise!—mayo actually helps *prevent* food from spoiling. Commercial mayonnaise is almost always made with vinegar and its acidity slows the growth of bacteria while increasing the sandwich's deliciousness. Win/win! (Unless we're talking about cholesterol.)

Of course, the mom on the field trip had actually made her daughter a peanut butter and jelly sandwich, which probably won't go bad until April 12, 2027. But now you know that mayo is okay-o.

Sudden Infant Death Syndrome (SIDS)

Sudden Infant Death Syndrome—SIDS—is a devastating disease, but the first thing to remember is that it is also rare, affecting about one baby in two thousand. We sometimes forget how very safe childhood is now compared to any other time in history. Abe Lincoln had four children, only one of whom made it to adulthood, and that was not an unusual track record back then. Even in the last hundred years, the infant mortality rate has plunged, from 111 children per 1,000 in 1915, to 26 per 1,000 in 1960, to 6.3 in 1,000 today. Yes, as recently as when we were kids, more or less, four times more children died in infancy than do now. So when we worry about childhood illnesses, let's try to keep in mind how much better the odds have become in our favor.

I know—that's hard to do when all we hear are warnings (and you're about to hear another). But knock wood your kid was born recently and then read on.

"SIDS is a mysterious disease. Kids die for no apparent reason," says Sydney Spiesel, a pediatrician and professor at Yale Medical School. He has his theories about what may cause it, but there's only one thing he is certain about: *put your baby to sleep on its back.*

The statistics seem irrefutable on this point. In 1992, the United States began its first major campaign against stomach sleeping. By 1994, SIDS deaths were down by 15 to 20 percent.

How did the medical establishment come to discover this simple preventive measure? By studying the different rates of SIDS in different countries. "There are tremendously different rates around the world, and sometimes the rate rises or drops the second you cross the border," says Spiesel. "And sometimes the rates would change dramatically in a country. So, for instance, the rate was pretty constant in Holland then suddenly, in a period of a year or so, it dramatically rose and everybody was scratching their heads."

What changed?

It was all "tremendously mysterious," Spiesel admits, "until we had an experiment in nature. That experiment occurred in Australia and New Zealand where, if anything, they have an excess of two things: Rabbits and sheep. It was almost a crime if you didn't put a sheepskin in your baby's crib, because what could be more wonderful than a sheepskin? But they had a very high rate in both those countries of SIDS, and one of the things they noticed was that those who slept on sheepskins had much higher rates [of SIDS]. Then they discovered that sleeping on a sheepskin amplifies the risk of sleeping face down."

Sleeping face down on something soft like sheepskin tends to prevent a lot of "gas exchange"—that is, it prevents a lot of new air from reaching the baby's nose and mouth. Instead, the carbon dioxide gets concentrated. Although Spiesel still believes that we may yet discover a genetic component to SIDS, he also thinks the face-down babies who die of it may have suffered from breathing in too high a concentration of carbon dioxide.

As for what happened in Holland that pushed up SIDS deaths so dramatically, it turned out to be a popular pamphlet given to new parents recommending tummy sleep for their infants, says Spiesel, a mistake the country has, of course, long since corrected.

Other recommendations from Spiesel and the American Academy of Pediatrics include making sure that the crib mattress is firm, because a baby's nose could sink into softer bedding. For that same reason, keeping stuffed animals, baby bumpers, or even pillows in the crib is not recommended. If you want to go the distance, skip the blankie, too. (But we always used one. Come to think of it, we had totally unnecessary, puffy baby bumpers, too, as if our kids were pinballs.) In 2000, several of the biggest baby bedding retailers—Babies R Us, IKEA, JCPenney, Kmart, Lands' End, Sears, and Target—all vowed to display their cribs bare of soft bedding. Considering they probably forfeited a bundle in the sale of fluffy baby junk, that was pretty noble of them.

The peak time for SIDS is the first two to four months. By the time kids can turn over from back to front by themselves, says Spiesel, "It's not an issue any more." They're much safer. Just start them out each night on their backs "and don't throw a lot of crap in the bed."

Well said.

Sunscreen, Vitamin D, Skin Cancer, You Name It

The rules for using sunscreen almost defy you or your child to live a normal life. The American Academy of Pediatrics advises older children, for instance, to "limit sun exposure during the peak intensity hours—between 10 AM and 4 PM."

Gee, that doesn't cramp anyone's day, does it? Just scurry inside at ten and don't come out again till four. What a fun summer! Fire up the Cartoon Network!

Meantime, the academy also recommends that children wear sunscreen and reapply it after "swimming or sweating."

"Wait up, guys! I'm glistening with perspiration! Gotta reapply the SPF 15!"

Have those words ever been uttered by a nonfictional child? Maybe if the kid had suffered a severe sunburn. But this is beyond the behavior of most real children, who consider sunscreen a gloppy form of cooties.

Anyway, as it turns out, maybe that's not so bad. Because the academy's newest worry is *rickets*! The bone-softening disease kids get when they don't get enough vitamin D! The vitamin we get from . . . sunshine!

Because of "recommendations regarding sun avoidance," reads an article in the journal *Pediatrics*, there have been "increasing numbers of reports of rickets in Western industrialized nations," and the reason for this may well be, "the excessive use of sunscreen."

Excessive?! Who told us to use it in the first place? Arghhhh!

So children are now instructed to get about fifteen minutes of unmitigated sun during the spring, winter, and fall, and to cover up the rest of the time. And that, I must wimpily admit, is my "official" recommendation to you, too. But unofficially, what I do is try to get my kids to put on some sunscreen in the morning if they're going to be outside most of the day, and wear hats.

Skin cancer is a reality, but it is not a childhood disease. It's something that usually develops later on—same as heart disease can, if your kid never gets out and runs around, and grows up to become a couch carrot. (I'm so sick of the word potato.) And then there's the no-sun-leads-to-rickets thing.

All in all, if you can avoid sunburns—great. But the idea of avoiding the great outdoors in the delectable Oreo middle of the day is like saying, "Avoid childhood so you can become an adult." Let us repeat:

Arghhhh.

Teen Sex (Yes, Kids, We Know You're Reading This. Now Come and Ask Us All About Contraception)

The good news? You don't have to have "The Talk."

The slightly more daunting news? Turns out you have to have talk after talk after *talk*. It's not just a one-shot deal.

The good news about the slightly daunting news? When you do start having these talks with your kids, you can totally screw up and it's OK. Because now that you know you're going to have, God help you, a zillion talks with your kids about sex, love, and body parts, you don't have to worry that if you don't present everything perfectly, they're going to end up like Jamie Lynn Spears (or what's-his-name the dad).

So when should these chats begin?

Planned Parenthood recommends you start talking to your kids about sex when they're preteens, because by middle school some kids will begin fooling around, and by high school, forget it. The latest numbers from the National Campaign to Prevent Teen and Unplanned Pregnancy found that in 2005, 46 percent of kids in high school had had sex at least once. That's down from 54 percent in 1991. But we're still talking about almost half of all high schoolers.

Doesn't simply talking to kids about sex increase the chances that they'll go and do it?

No.

Truly, statistically, it does not. I asked. And even keeping some condoms available doesn't make kids run out and use them, any more than keeping umbrellas around makes it rain.

Billy Crystal once said that he wouldn't mind his daughters having sex—as long as they wait till he's dead. But even if you preach abstinence before marriage (or parental death), your conversations should still cover pregnancy and sexually transmitted diseases and birth control. How come? Because if your children *do* have sex sooner than you'd like them to—something that I hear has happened at least once or twice in human history—you want them to be safe. So instead of just hoping they sit tight, your job is to give them the information that some day, when you're not around (or maybe you're upstairs watching Leno), they can use. Planned Parenthood calls this approach "Abstinence Plus."

Plus nonabstinence, I guess.

Anyway, one thing you can remind your children is that even if they do decide to have sex, they can always go back to abstaining whenever they want. (Sort of like when Madonna went through that I'm-a-proper-English-children's-author phase.) Also remind your children that you love them no matter what and that they can come to you with any embarrassing questions they have.

About sex, that is. Not about why you're wearing that outfit.

The Woods, Playing In

"The woods are lovely, dark and deep."

Thank you, Bob Frost, thanks a heap.

Thanks for that "Stopping by Woods on a Snowy Evening" poem, reinforcing the fact that woods are dark and deep. Now we'll never let our kids play in them, even though there's something almost transcendent about kids connecting with nature.

"Nature Deficit Syndrome" is the name Richard Louv uses in his book *Last Child in the Woods* to describe the sad situation of kids today, most destined never to explore anything wilder than a Chuck E. Cheese.

One story in Louv's book concerns a couple of bored, cranky kids whose fed-up parents send them out to a field behind the house with the order, "Don't come back for two hours!" Well, the kids come back *several* hours later, excited and happy. That's because there's so much to discover in nature, from bugs to trees to soaring attention levels. One study at the University of Illinois found that kids with Attention Deficit Hyperactivity Disorder had fewer symptoms after playing in nature than they had after playing video games.

So why don't we send kids out to explore more?

"The woods seem chaotic," says Robert Bixler, a professor at South Carolina's Clemson University who trains future forest rangers. We're used to either urban playgrounds or suburban lawns, both of which bear about as much resemblance to actual forests as snow domes bear to Antarctica. The woods are unfamiliar.

Generally, unfamiliar things are scary, and that's especially true when worrywarts keep warning us about them. One parenting magazine piece, "The Great Outdoors," ran with the subhead, "We've pulled together the gear and accessories you need for a fun (and totally safe) day in the sun."

Like you couldn't possibly go outside and expect to be safe with your child without four pages of safety precautions and a truckload of junk—excuse me—"gear," including an insulated stroller organizer to keep baby's juice cold and a $590 bike trailer.

Before the fifth graders at my sons' school go on their overnight to a nature preserve, they receive a ten-page xerox detailing every possible danger, from poison sumac to wolves to bears to "bald-faced hornets" who "build nests shaped like footballs." How inviting! And I'm sure kids get really psyched to hike after they read that whole paragraph on "what a bee sting looks and feels like."

Nonetheless, even the super-cautious school realizes that being in nature is important for kids. It nurtures curiosity and independence and a connectedness to time and the earth and all the stuff it's impossible to talk about without waxing crunchy.

Think back on your own childhood, and chances are you'll recall spending some very rewarding time in nature. Find some again now, even if it's only the edge of a playground where the weeds are growing wild. Give your little explorers guidelines about how far they can go, give them a tick check when they return home (although ticks are only active when it's warm out, so in winter climes this is not an issue), and heck—these days you can even give them a phone.

The woods are lovely, dark and deep.

Have a great day and wait for the beep.

Walking to School (or at Least the Bus Stop)

Here's one of those ironic facts that'll haunt you tomorrow morning if you have a child heading off to school. Do you know what percentage of kids hit by cars near schools are hit by cars driven by parents dropping *their* kids off because they're afraid of *them* getting hit by cars?

Half! Fifty percent! One out of two.

So if everyone just walked to school, already we'd see a 50 percent reduction in the number of children hit by cars near school!

Walking to school used to be so commonplace, it wasn't even up for discussion. Forty years ago, 66 percent of U.S. children walked or biked to school, says Ian Thomas, executive director of a Missouri-based pro-walking group called the PedNet Coalition. (I'd change that name, buddy.) Now the number of kids walking is down to about 10 percent.

Some of this can be attributed to schools built on cheap land at the edge of town from the sixties onwards—big schools that take kids from such a wide catchment that it is too far for most to walk—and also to the stupid suburban idea that since we all have cars, who needs sidewalks? No sidewalks, no safe routes to school, no walkers.

But there are still plenty of neighborhood schools that are reachable. And yet the Free-Range Kids site gets a ton of letters like this: "I can see my children's school from my bedroom window and I let my nine-year-old walk his sister to school. She's six. Some parents think that is crazy. My neighbor drives her children to school every morning."

What that neighbor has yet to realize is that if kids started walking again, everyone would be better off, thanks to less pollution, less traffic, fewer accidents, and fitter—as opposed to fatter—kids. And by the way: kids who get their morning exercise may even do better in school, having gotten their ya-yas out along the way. Children are supposed to get an hour of exercise a day, but most don't. I won't even go into the long-term health implications. (Well—yes I will, really fast: diabetesheartdiseaseobesity.) So let's just assume that with all the advantages of walking, parents must be driving either because they've simply gotten into the habit or because they think that walking is dangerous.

Is it?

In many neighborhoods, it doesn't have to be. The two big fears of parents are that their children will be hurt by traffic or snatched by a predator. There is a way to prevent both of these. It's called the "walking school bus."

A walking school bus is like a carpool without the car (or pool). You and some other parents get together and agree that you will each take turns walking to school and, like a bus, pick up the kids in your group along the way. Thus there is always a parent around to supervise street crossings and keep those pedophiles at bay. (Read the chapter Strangers with Candy to see how few pedophiles are actually lying in wait.)

Your job is to find a safe route and to teach your children how to cross streets. But as the weeks go by, it is not unusual for the children to start walking by themselves, the way we did way back when. It's not that big a deal!

Then there are a couple of other things parents can do to make the route safer that parents didn't do in my day. And these would have really helped my sister.

In our quiet Chicago suburb she was often tormented on her way to grammar school by two neighborhood bullies who teased her, sometimes sexually, may they rot in hell (along with everyone else's bullies). Pedestrian safety researcher David Levinger suggests that a way to cut down on this kind of threat is to not entirely bow out of your child's commute when she goes by herself. Sometimes, on no particular schedule, join your child. Let all the kids in the neighborhood see that you are part of your child's life. Lend your heft.

Second, you want to let your children know that they can talk to you about any problems they have along their route. I don't recall my sister ever confiding her misery to my parents, or my parents asking her, "Everything cool?" That might have made a big difference.

All of these suggestions, by the way, work just as well with letting your child walk to and from the bus stop.

Free-Range Parents are not hands off. We give our children the tools to be safe and independent, and we listen to them too. And then, once all the stars align, we let them walk (or skip or bike or hop) to school.

But the hopping gets old fast.

Zoo Animals (in Cracker Form and Otherwise)

If you're worried about zoo animals as cookie or cracker snacks, please see, "Choking on Food and All the Other Little Things Around the House."

If you're worried about zoo animals and *children* as snacks, please see "Animals, Being Eaten By."

If you're worried about lead in zoo animals from China, please read "Lead Paint, Lead Toys, and Lead Everything from China."

But if you're worried about whether your child is allergic to zoo animals, you're on your own. Sorry.

Strangers with Candy

Even the Folks Who Put the Faces on the Milk Cartons Aren't Too Worried

Death by abduction. It is the mother of all worries—and the worry of all mothers. And dads.

If you have skipped straight to this topic, don't feel bad. That's what the TV news does too. Anyway, there are no penalties for not reading this book in order (other than one brief "What would your English teacher say!? Is this how you read *The Scarlet Letter,* too?").

On the other hand, if you have come to this chapter the old-fashioned way, by reading the words that led up to it, hello again! You will have heard a couple of the abduction statistics before, but this is where they all come together as we confront the great fear. Starting now.

The grandmother was sitting in the allergist's waiting room, reading her paper with a magnifying glass. A boy, around age three, came up to her.

"He was just this darling little boy and he wanted to look through the magnifying glass," recalls the grandma, Rochelle Jewel Shapiro. She was about to hand it to him when his mother rushed over and scooped him up, exclaiming, "He has to learn fast not to talk to strangers!"

What. An. Idiot.

Sorry. I'd like to be more sympathetic to that mom, who was only trying to keep her child safe, as are we all, etc., etc., etc. But has she given one *iota* of thought to the lesson she's teaching him? A lesson that boils down to "Don't trust anybody, ever, under any circumstances"? It's like those airport screeners who make the ninety-five-year-old with the bun and the cane stand there and get wanded.

That's not the way to keep anyone safe. And that "Don't trust anyone!" lesson could conceivably end up making that little boy *less* safe (not to mention terrified of old ladies). Imagine if, against all odds—and I'm about to tell you just how long those odds are— some horrible guy *does* come up one day and say, "Hi, little fella. Mommy sent me to get you." Presto—he mentioned mom, so he's not a stranger anymore. He grabs the boy even while, just a few feet away with her back turned, a grandma sits reading her paper. Will the little boy scream, "Hey lady! Help! Put down the magni- fying glass and call the police!" Or will he not say anything, be- cause she's a stranger, and Mommy said never to talk to them?

"Don't talk to strangers" is one of the most useless pieces of ad- vice ever foisted on us to foist on our children. And I'm not the only one who thinks so.

"Our message is exactly the one you're trying to convey. We have been trying to debunk the myth of stranger danger," says Ernie Allen.

What's stunning about this statement is that Allen is the head of the National Center for Missing and Exploited Children. The or- ganization John Walsh helped found after his son was killed. The organization that runs 1–800-THE LOST. *The organization that put the missing kids' pictures on the milk cartons and didn't tell us that most of them were runaways or abducted by family members*. And although I believe that his organization is one of the reasons we are all so out of our minds with abduction fear, it turns out that Allen and I are in heated agreement that parents are worried about the wrong prob- lem and giving out the wrong solution.

"Our message to parents is you don't have to live in fear, you don't have to feel you have to lock your children in a room," says Allen. What you do have to do, he says, is talk to them about how to handle themselves confidently, among people they know and people they don't.

Let's talk about the likelihood of abduction first, and then we'll talk about what to teach your kids. (And why I ended up thinking Allen is great.)

Having pretty much dispatched with diphtheria, whooping cough, polio, TB, scurvy, smallpox, consumption, cholera, typhoid, scrofula, Spanish flu, malaria, yellow fever, and the bubonic plague—at least here in the comfort of the First World—the towering parental fear is now the thought of one's child being kidnapped, carried off, and killed by a creep in a van. (Vans are in need of some major PR.) This particular scenario is known, in the juvenile justice world, as "stereotypical kidnapping." And even though it feels as if it's happening all the time—and on TV, it is—it's actually exceedingly rare and getting rarer.

As of 1999, the latest year for which we have statistics, the number of U.S. children abducted this way was 115. Of those, 40 percent were killed, bringing the total to about fifty, or 1 in 1.5 million. But the number of abductions may actually be even lower today than it was in 1999, because crimes against children have been plummeting since the early nineties. Homicides of children under age fourteen were down 36 percent from 1993 to 2005; teen homicides were down 60 percent. And juvenile sex crimes were down a whopping 79 *percent*, according to the Crimes Against Children Research Center. Imagine a graph of Hummer sales in 2008, or Miami condo prices, or birthday cards to Bernie Madoff. That's what a graph of crime over the past fifteen years looks like: an unbelievably dramatic jackknife down.

Crime peaked around 1992 or 1993, so if you grew up any time in the seventies or eighties as it was ramping up, there is no need to feel that times now are less safe. As I've noted before in this book, crime has returned to the levels of the early seventies and continues to go down.

That is all phenomenally great news, and there are several reasons for it, ranging from more cops to better prosecution of sex offenders to less tolerance of abuse within the family. (Thank you, daytime talk shows!) Cell phones are probably also to thank, because as the number of phones has gone up, the number of crimes has gone down. And we should also thank our medical and social work system for getting more troubled people onto psychiatric meds. This may be the "sleeper" reason fewer crimes are being committed, says sociologist David Finkelhor: the criminally insane are feeling less insane and hence, less criminal. So hooray for progress from the streets to the courts to the clinics! Let's hear it for society working!

But, of course, you never do. Hear about society working, that is. "Mellowed-out criminal uninterested in snatching local child, and even if he did, greater police presence would probably prevent it" is just not a ratings grabber. At least not compared to "Child snatched off scooter!"

We've hashed out the media problem already, so I won't start in again. I'm just trying to explain why this incredible good news about crimes against kids seems to contradict everything you've read, heard, and seen. But there are two more reasons why all this good news may not be at all reassuring to you:

1. It's lovely that abductions are down. But what if that 1 in 1.5 million is YOUR KID?

2. It's lovely that abductions are down. But what if that 1 in 1.5 million is MY KID?

That's how everyone thinks—including me. And I've been thinking that way even more, ever since the world decided to weigh in on whether or not I was an irresponsible jerk to let my nine-year-old ride the subway alone. Usually after I replied to my detractors by rattling off all my safety stats, the person would probe,

"But what if that one was *your* kid?" followed by, "How would you ever forgive yourself?"

Answer: I wouldn't.

Of course I wouldn't! But what was so upsetting about these questions was the notion behind them: that I'd deliberately put my son in harm's way—and didn't give a hoot—when actually I was allowing him to do something that was extremely safe. And confidence building and competence building too.

Then one day I got an e-mail that deserves the Nobel Prize for Clobbering Parental Hysteria. (Stockholm, get busy.) It suggested that from now on, whenever anyone asks, "How could you possibly let your child get around on his own? Wouldn't you feel terrible if something happened?" you respond, "How could you possibly let your kids get in the car with you? Wouldn't you feel awful if they were in a crash?"

After all, a child is *forty times more likely to die as a passenger in a car crash* than to be kidnapped and murdered by a stranger.

Using this wonderful e-mailer's strategy, you could even respond, "How could you possibly make your kids stay inside after school instead of letting them wander around on their own? Wouldn't you feel awful if they were burned to a crisp?" After all, there are about fifty children killed by kidnappers each year, but *ten times that number are killed by fires at home*.

And by the way, "How could you possibly get your kids a pool?" After all, they are *almost twenty times more likely to drown* than to be kidnapped and murdered. And "How could you possibly let your children visit a relative?" After all, they are *eighty or ninety times more likely to be molested by someone they know than* . . .

You get the idea. The point is not to make parents even more nervous about everything they do, every second, every place. It's to make them realize that a lot of our fears are off base. Things that we're familiar with, like driving, don't scare us, despite the odds. Meanwhile the stranger danger fear is so gruesome and out of the ordinary, it dominates our parenting lives even though it doesn't deserve to. You know that book they have for kids, *Go Away, Big Green Monster!?* We need one for adults: *Go Away, Unlikely Predator Scenario!*

The good news: there really is a way to make the predator fear go away. The better news: it will actually make your kid safer, too. It's called empowerment.

Glen Evans is a police officer and father of four outside of Dayton, Ohio. About five years ago, his four-year-old asked him anxiously, "Daddy, what if a bad guy comes and says, 'I'm going to do this, this, and this!'?" And he proceeded to act out a series of Power Ranger moves.

Teachable-moment Daddy replied, "Well, what if somebody came up to you and said, 'Hey, I have some puppies in the car, why don't you come with me?' What would you do then?"

The excited boy said, "I'd run!"

The excited dad said, "Fine. Run!"

So the boy ran around the house and came back jazzed and happy. Evans was equally jazzed. As a cop, he realized he'd just taught his son a fine lesson: when an adult tries to get you into a car—run. But most parents are not cops and have no idea what to teach their kids about personal safety. The proverbial light bulb started hovering over Evans's head. He would go forth and teach the safety tips a cop knows!

So now that's what he does. His company is called ASSERT Super Kids and he teaches everyone from MOPS (Mothers of Pre-Schoolers) to tweens all about how to stay safe from creeps. He likens his lessons to the lessons cops get on how to use a gun. It's unlikely they'll ever need to use the weapon. But by knowing what to do in an emergency, they become not only prepared but confident. And we have confidence in them, too.

Evans's technique is visual and, above all, physical. It involves literally showing kids the lures a predator could use: a bag of candy, a leash that supposedly "proves" a guy is looking for his puppy.

Then he has the children practice the three things that could help them the most:

1. Throwing their hands in front of them like a stop sign.
2. Screaming at the top of their lungs, "No! Get away! You're not my dad!" "Your voice is your most effective crime-fighting tool," he tells them.
3. Running like hell.

By actually getting up and practicing those things, the kids feel ready for the worst. But it's not just them: the parents who are watching them get a surge of confidence, too. Public safety instructors liken this kind of training to the "Stop, drop, and roll" drill that kids get as part of fire safety instruction. Once again, it is extremely unlikely they'll ever need to use it, but—it's handy to have. And rather than creating more fear, it seems to help alleviate it. The more afraid we are of something, the more power it has over us. But the more prepared we are, the more power we get back. Training confers power.

One more thing Evans tries to convince the parents, by the way, is not to tell children, "Don't talk to strangers." "When you tell your children not to talk to a stranger, you are effectively removing hundreds of good people in the area who could be helping them," he says. Instead, Evans teaches the kids that

1. Most adults are good.
2. There are a few bad ones.
3. Most normal adults don't drive up and ask for help.
4. If they do, or if they bother you in any other way, you can ask any other nearby adult for help. And again, if you need to, scream, hit, and run.

The best piece of advice I heard while researching this topic comes from a psychotherapist named Michelle Maidenberg, and it's really simple: tell your kids they *can* talk to strangers. They can ask for help from strangers. What they should never do is *go off* with strangers.

Teach kids NEVER GO OFF WITH STRANGERS, even if those strangers say they have something nice to give you or need your help or were supposedly sent by Mom.

To fine-tune the message, you can tell your kids never to go off with anyone you haven't preapproved beforehand. Simple as that.

Over at the National Center for Missing and Exploited Children, Ernie Allen approves. "Probably no single case in the twenty-five years we've been here has had greater impact and unleashed a greater flood of calls than the case of eleven-year-old Carlie Brucia," he says, recalling the Florida case from 2004. "She was approached by this guy and it was captured by a video camera at a car wash, and the child ended up murdered. This was a very bright little girl, and what was so terrifying to parents was they saw how easily and how fast it happened. He said something to her and led her away. No resistance, no fighting back, no trying to run."

We still don't know what the killer—Joseph Smith—said to the girl, but at the time of this writing, he is on death row for the crime. Meantime, Allen's organization has studied hundreds of abductions that ended very differently: the victims got away. How?

"Overwhelmingly, by either running away or fighting back: yelling, kicking, pulling away, or attracting attention," Allen says. So that's exactly what the center encourages kids to understand: you have a *right* to call attention to yourself, to resist a grown-up, to stand up for yourself, to be impolite, and to ask others for help.

Interestingly, says Allen, these turn out to be the very "same techniques you'd use to resist peer pressure over drugs or bullies or gangs."

Let's talk about those bullies for a second. Although parents most fear the man-with-van, the greatest number of young people are harassed and harmed by people they know, often other young people. Of the fifty-eight thousand people under age seventeen who go missing for more than an hour, having been taken or seduced away, almost two-thirds are between the ages of fifteen and seventeen. Most of them are girls. And most of them went off—by force or foolishness—with friends, relatives, boyfriends, or acquaintances.

This is not to minimize the danger they're in or to blame them for bad judgment. It's to point out that self-esteem and self-confidence come into play here just as much as they do with a younger kid approached by a pervert on the playground.

Teach your children, including your teens, that they have a right to say NO to anyone who wants them to do anything they don't want to do (except homework). Back this up by letting them know you will support and love them even if they do end up doing something ill thought out. (Or even stupid.) That way they'll be able to confide in you, and you can give them guidance.

Finkelhor adds, as a practical matter, that he would equip teenage girls, especially, with pepper spray. And he'd have kids carry cell phones, so that they can alert you or another adult, or call 911. Make sure they know about 911.

"It's not enough to talk to them thirty minutes a year," says Allen, on the subject of safety instruction. "You need to role play. You need to practice, so when the time comes, they can act. And you don't do it in a scary way, because scary doesn't work. You try to scare the kids to death, what you end up doing is you paralyze them. So the whole essence is you empower children."

Although I had my misgivings about Allen's center because it has made abductions the main focal point of parental fears and has led to all sorts of unintended consequences (like parents driving their kids to school and keeping them cooped up afterward, isolated, and usually glued to a screen), I ended up with great respect for his organization. It has helped countless children, even if it scared the bejeezus out of a bunch of us too. As it turns out, Allen and I actually share the very same goal: happy, safe kids who are confident out and about in the world.

Free-Range Kids, in fact.

REAL WORLD

The Whole Time He Was in There I Was Sweating

Gaelle, a Free-Range Mom, writes:

> My son is 5 years old. A couple of months ago we were at the airport and he needed to use the restroom, but he insisted on using the boy's one. I gave in—the line in the ladies restroom was pretty long.
>
> The whole time he was in there, I was sweating out of fear that a child molester had been waiting for that opportunity and was in that same bathroom, about to hurt my child. It seemed to take forever for him to come out, so I asked a gentleman walking out if he had seen a little boy in there. He smiled at me and replied, "Yes. He is washing his hands at the moment. He needed help to reach the soap."
>
> WOW! My 5-year-old actually remembered to wash his hands?
>
> He came out of the restroom, clean hands, a huge smile on his face. And I started breathing again.

Going Free Range

Free-Range Baby Step: Let your school-age child go into a public bathroom alone. Wait outside.

Free-Range Brave Step: Do what the safety teachers all say to do: teach your children never to go off with someone they don't know. Then practice this. Have them throw their hands up as stop signs, scream "Get away!" and literally run off. Try to make it kind of fun. After my friend's daughter was on a public bus where a guy grabbed another girl's behind, my friend had the gaggle of schoolgirls practice shouting, "Get your hands off of me!" at the top of their lungs. She made it into a sort of cheer. Come to think of it, wouldn't it be cool if real cheerleaders started practicing cheers like that? "Two, four, six, eight! Back off or I'll amputate!" "Hey hey! Ho ho! Copping feels has got to go!" I would *love* to hear a whole stadium cheering along. Talk about empowerment.

Giant Leap for Free-Range Kind: If abductions are still gnawing at you, do something to make the world a safer place. Call your local police and volunteer to host a safety meeting at your home. Enroll your kids or the whole family in a self-defense class. Or at least make up a new cheer. Taking action breaks down the fear.

While you're at it, teach your children a lesson about how to get help if ever they need it: by talking to strangers.

Conclusion

The Other Problem That Has No Name—and Its Solution

"The problem lay buried, unspoken, for many years in the minds of American children. It was a strange stirring, a sense of dissatisfaction, a yearning that children suffered. . . . Each suburban child struggled with it alone . . . afraid to ask even the silent question: Is this all?"

So begins the revolutionary classic, *The Feminine Mystique*. Except that I have taken the liberty of substituting "child" and "children" for "women" and "wife."

As you may recall, *The Feminine Mystique* first introduced us to "the problem that had no name"—a problem that boiled down to housewives going bonkers with boredom. They knew they were supposed to find fulfillment in their lovely homes and gleaming appliances—and many did. But many others longed to get out in the world, use their talents, stretch. They wanted to be treated like competent human beings, not helpless kittens. But at the time Betty Friedan was writing, 1963, just twenty years after women had rolled up their sleeves and riveted the bombers that won World War II, they were told, Sweetheart, what are you talking about? It's a man's world out here. Too dangerous for you. Too difficult. You've got everything you could possibly want right there at home. So stay there. Inside. Safe.

Same thing we are telling kids now.

Yes, of course, there is a difference between grown women and young children, but there is also something strangely familiar about the idea of suddenly deciding that the outside world is way too dangerous for a certain segment of the population. A segment that had been doing just fine in the outside world until that point. A segment abruptly informed that it could no longer do anything on its own—and that all this restriction was for its own good.

As I've said throughout this book, childhood really has changed since we were kids. I know all middle-aged people at some point start saying, "In my day . . ." That's how you know they're middle-aged. It's like a verbal paunch. But in our day, kids *did* walk to school. Parents did *not* drive them home from the bus stop. Kids *did* play in the park without anyone hovering, and they *did* stay out until dark.

That has changed not just in the United States, but throughout the English-speaking world. Australian children get stared at when they ride the bus alone. Canadian kids stay inside playing video games. I heard from a dad in Ireland who lets his eleven-year-old play in the local park, unsupervised, and now a mom down the street won't let her son go to their house. She thinks the dad is reckless. And there was a great article in the English paper *The Daily Mail*, "How Children Lost the Right to Roam in Four Generations."

The reporter interviewed four generations of the same family. The eighty-eight-year-old great-grandpa, George, used to walk six miles to his favorite fishing hole, alone, at age eight. His son, now sixty-three, played in the woods a mile from his home when he was eight. His daughter, at that same age, walked half a mile to school. Now her son, age eight, is driven to school. He is not allowed to leave his block, and neither are any of his friends. Most of them don't even leave their yards.

And here's a letter I got over Christmas break from an American:

I'm fifteen right now and get pretty much no freedom. I'm limited to what's inside the house and the backyard. I can't even go as far as the sidewalk—I might be "abducted or killed." I used to walk to a bus stop, but my dad said it was too dangerous, so he started driving me there (it's a five-minute walk!), and eventually he just started driving me to school. Today, after playing video games for two hours or so, I went downstairs and realized that the only things I could do there were eat and watch TV. Watching TV, playing video games, and eating junk food are fun and all, but after even just a few days, it gets old. (I've been on winter break for half a week now.) I don't want my kids (if I ever even have kids) to live like me at all.

It is the problem that has no name.

Childhood is supposed to be about discovering the world, not being held captive. It's not about having that world pointed out to you by a DVD or a video game or by your mom as you drive by. "See, honey? That's called a 'forest.' Can you spell *forest?*"

We want our children to have a childhood that's magical and enriched, but I'll bet that your best childhood memories involve something you were thrilled to do by yourself. *These* are childhood's magic words: "I did it myself!"

It is time we gave them back to our kids.

Childhood independence has become taboo, even though our world is no less safe than it was twenty or thirty years ago. The ground has not gradually gotten harder under the jungle gym. The bus stops have not crept further from home. Crime is actually lower than it was when most of us were growing up. So there is no reality-based reason that children today should be treated as more helpless and vulnerable than we were when we were young.

Like the housewives of the fifties, today's children need to be liberated. Unlike the housewives of the fifties, the children can't do it themselves.

Though I'd love to see hordes of kids gathering for meetings, staging protests, and burning their baby knee pads—and maybe they will—it is really up to us parents to start renormalizing childhood. That begins with us realizing how scared we've gotten, even of ridiculously remote dangers. Overheard, for example, at the American Museum of Natural History: "Hurry up, kids, stay right behind me! I don't want you kidnapped!" That's the kind of thing we have to get over.

We also have to get over the fear of letting our children fail. They don't have to spend every moment getting good at something. They don't have to be pro soccer players for us to love them. And if they actually go ahead and lose at soccer, they don't have to receive a trophy. One midwestern dad had to explain to his daughter why the award she brought home was for "Second Winner"! A second winner, dad gingerly explained, is what we used to call "the loser."

We have to be less afraid of nature and more willing to embrace the idea that some rashes and bites are a fair price to pay in exchange for appreciating the wonder of a cool-looking rock or an unforgettable fern. And I say this having gone through a huge bout of poison ivy with one son that had his legs looking like a relief map of Mars.

When we watch TV, we have to remind ourselves that its job is to terrify and disgust us so that we'll keep watching in horror. It is doing an excellent job on both fronts.

We have to be willing to stand up to equally terrifying "experts," even the self-declared ones in our own parenting groups, who bring in the latest study as if it's a moose they just shot. "Look! I just found out that [fill in the blank] is extremely bad for children/babies/nursing moms/pets." We have to remember that we live in safe times with lots of safeguards and laws and medical advances that have made childhood less dangerous than at any other time in the history of human beings.

We have to learn to remind the other parents who think we're being careless when we loosen our grip that we are actually trying to teach our children how to get along in the world, and that we believe this is our job. A child who can fend for himself is a lot safer than one forever coddled, because the coddled child will not have Mom or Dad around all the time, even though they act as if he will. Maybe that's even the plan. Maybe they don't mind raising a kid who thinks he's helpless without them.

And on top of all this, we have to give our kids the tools they need to go Free Range. Teach them about bike safety and bad guys and traffic signals and how to ask for help and how to handle disappointment and what to do if they get lost and all the things parents have always had to teach their kids. Or at least they did until recently, when they decided they could just do everything *for* them instead.

I write this in a kind of shaky mood because I just got a call from the police. I put Izzy, now ten, on a half-hour train ride out to his friend's house this morning. It sounds like I'm a recidivist, but really: his friend's family was waiting at the other end to pick him up, and he's done this a dozen times already. It is a straight shot on a commuter railroad. This particular time, however, the conductor found it outrageous that a ten-year-old should be traveling alone, and summoned the police, who arrived as my son disembarked.

When the officer phoned me at home, I told him the truth (while my heart stood still): we had actually inquired of the railroad what age a child can travel alone and were told there was no specific regulation about this.

The officer said no problem and wished me Merry Christmas, because that's what today is. And off my son went with his friend's family.

But this is the world we're living in. One where a ten-year-old can't do anything by himself without it being cause for alarm, or even arrest. Later I looked up the official rules: a child only has to be eight to ride alone on the railroad *or* subway. Good rule.

Independence should be cause for celebration. Recall the story in Commandment 8 of the Italian orphan Rocco, a kid growing up a hundred years ago: how he escaped a Fagin-like taskmaster at age eleven and found his way to a family of fishermen and worked for them until he got himself to America—all by age sixteen. You can bet no conductor arrested him for traveling on his own. Adults knew then what we have forgotten today. Kids are competent. Kids are capable. Kids deserve freedom, responsibility, and a chance to be part of this world, not cooped up like, well . . . chickens.

In our enlightenment, we have finally returned to some lucky, clucking, real, live chickens the old-fashioned, God-given freedom to range. Our children deserve no less. Long live Free-Range Kids.

Sources

Dear sources aficionado: As a longtime newspaper reporter, I gathered much of my information the old-fashioned way, through interviews (and the less old-fashioned way, through e-mail chats). If I did not identify a book or a study as the source of my facts in the text, it's because I got the information from a human being. The published sources I used are as follows.

Introduction

Baker, Al. "Crime Numbers Keep Dropping Across the City." *New York Times*, Dec. 31, 2005, Section A, p. 1.

Crimes Against Children Research Center (http://www.unh.edu/ccrc/).

Crimes Against Children Research Center crime trends statistics (http://www.unh.edu/ccrc/Trends/index.html).

Crimes Against Children Research Center kidnapping statistics (http://www.unh.edu/ccrc/kidnapping/).

Finkelhor, David. "The Great Interpersonal Violence Decline." Presentation at the American Psychological Association Interpersonal Violence Summit, Bethesda, Md., February 2008.

Finkelhor, David, Heather Hammer, and Andrea J. Sedlak. "Nonfamily Abducted Children: National Estimates and Characteristics." Prepared for the U.S. Department of Justice. (http://www.ncjrs.gov/pdffiles1/ojjdp/196467.pdf).

U.S. Department of Justice, Federal Bureau of Investigation. "Crime in the United States." 2007. (http://www.fbi.gov/ucr/cius2007/data/table_01.html).

Commandment 1: Know When to Worry

Clements, Rhonda. "An Investigation of the Status of Outdoor Play." *Contemporary Issues in Early Childhood*, 2004, 5(1), 68–80.
Crimes Against Children Research Center (http://www.unh.edu/ccrc/).
PedNet Coalition (www.pednet.org).
Russell, Cheryl. *Bet You Didn't Know: Hundreds of Intriguing Facts About Living in the USA*. Amherst, N.Y.: Prometheus Books, 2008.

Commandment 2: Turn Off the News

Cairns, Warwick. *How to Live Dangerously*. London: Macmillan, 2008.
Centers for Disease Control and Prevention. "Water-Related Injuries: Fact Sheet." (http://www.cdc.gov/ncipc/factsheets/drown.htm).
Gardner, Daniel. *The Science of Fear*. New York: Dutton, 2008.
Gill, Tim. *No Fear: Growing Up in a Risk Averse Society*. London: Calouste Gulbenkian Foundation, 2007.
National Highway Traffic Administration Safety statistics (NHTSA.dot.gov/People/PeopleAllVictims.aspx).
National Highway Traffic Administration Safety statistics, crunched by Fatality Analysis Reporting System (http://www-fars.nhtsa.dot.gov/People/PeopleAllVictims.aspx).

Commandment 3: Avoid Experts

Barrett, Stephen, MD (quackwatch.com).
Deerwester, Karen. *The Potty Training Answer Book: Practical Answers to the Top 200 Questions Parents Ask*. Naperville, Ill.: Sourcebooks, 2007.
Dimerman, Sara. *Am I a Normal Parent?* Long Island City, N.Y.: Hatherleigh Press, 2008.
Fields, Denise, and Ari Brown. *Baby 411*. (3rd ed.) Boulder, Colo.: Windsor Peak Press, 2007.
Gomi, Taro, and Amanda Mayer Stinchecum. *Everyone Poops*. La Jolla, Calif.: Kane/Miller, 2001.
Karp, Harvey. *The Happiest Toddler on the Block: How to Eliminate Tantrums and Raise a Patient, Respectful, and Cooperative One- to Four-Year-Old*. (Rev. ed.) New York: Bantam, 2008.

McDonald, Libby. *The Toxic Sandbox: The Truth About Environmental Toxins and Our Children's Health*. New York: Perigee Trade, 2007.

Murkoff, Heidi, and Sharon Mazel. *What to Expect When You're Expecting*. (4th ed.) New York: Workman, 2008.

Spock, Benjamin, and Robert Needlman. *Dr. Spock's Baby and Child Care*. (8th ed.) New York: Pocket Books, 2004.

Swartz, Jillian (http://thefamilygroove.com).

Commandment 4: Boycott Baby Knee Pads

Babies R Us (babiesrus.com).

Baby-Safe Inc (http://www.babysafeamerica.com/BSA_About.html).

Centers for Disease Control and Prevention. "Child Passenger Safety Fact Sheet." (http://www.cdc.gov/ncipc/factsheets/childpas.htm).

Linn, Susan. *The Case for Make Believe*. New York: New Press, 2008.

Linn, Susan. *Consuming Kids: Protecting Our Children from the Onslaught of Marketing and Advertising*. New York: Anchor Books, 2005.

Christoper, Maura. "Let's Rock!" *Parents Magazine*, Oct. 2008, pp. 136–142.

Onestepahead.com.

Paul, Pamela. *Parenting, Inc.: How We Are Sold on $800 Strollers, Fetal Education, Baby Sign Language, Sleeping Coaches, Toddler Couture, and Diaper Wipe Warmers—and What It Means for Our Children*. New York: Times Books, 2008.

Thudguard.com.

U.S. Consumer Product Safety Commission. "CPSC Warns: Pools Are Not the Only Drowning Danger at Home for Kids—Data Show Other Hazards Cause More Than 100 Residential Child Drowning Deaths Annually." May 23, 2002. (http://www.cpsc.gov/cpscpub/prerel/prhtml02/02169.html).

Commandment 5: Don't Think Like a Lawyer

Fanelli, James, and Mike Scholl. "Base Accusation: Injured Kid's Mom Sues 'Slide Fool' Coach." *New York Post*, May 20, 2007, p. 3.

Howard, Philip K., chair of Common Good. Congressional testimony on liability and childhood to the judiciary of the U.S. House of Representatives, June 22, 2004. (http://commongood.org/assets/attachments/80.pdf).

Mahoney, Dennis. "Lawsuit Threat Forces NU to Ban Evening Legion Games." *Evanston Review*, June 26, 2008. (http://www.pioneerlocal.com/evanston/sports/highschools/1024046,ev-legionsun-062608-s1.article).

Michigan Lawsuit Abuse Watch (www.mlaw.org).

"Past Winners of M-Law's Wacky Warning Label Contests." (http://www.mlaw
.org/wwl/pastwinners.html).

"School Principal Survey Reveals Fear of Liability Limits Educational Opportunities for America's Children." Survey conducted in conjunction with
the National Association of Secondary School Principals and the National School Boards Association's Council of School Attorneys,
2007. (http://www.atra.org/show/91).

"Schools Keep Our Kids Safe from Hula-Hoops." *Chicago Sun Times*, Sept. 5,
2008, features section, p. 32.

Commandment 6: Ignore the Blamers

"Illinois Babysitting Laws." Labor Log Talk blog (blog.laborlawtalk.com/2006/
11/10/Illinois-babysitting-laws/).

National Child Care Information Center, U.S. Department of Health and
Human Services. "Children Home Alone and Babysitter Age Guidelines," Oct. 14, 2008. (http://nccic.acf.hhs.gov/poptopics/homealone
.html).

Singer, Jen (MommaSaid.net).

Commandment 7: Eat Chocolate

Henderson, Tom. "Be Very Afraid, You Giant Wimp." *Lewiston Morning Tribune*,
Oct. 25, 2006, p. 6A.

"Man Ordered to Take Down His Halloween Decorations Because They Are
Too Scary." *Daily Mail* (England), Oct. 29, 2008. (http://www.daily
mail.co.uk/news/article-1081614/Man-ordered-Halloween
-decorations-scary.html).

Safety.com.

Commandment 8: Study History

Heffernan, Virginia. "Sweeping the Clouds Away." *New York Times Magazine*,
Nov. 18, 2007, p. 34. (http://www.nytimes.com/2007/11/18/
magazine/18wwln-medium-t.html).

Lou and Lou Safety Patrol. Playhouse Disney. (http://atv.disney.go.com/
playhouse/safetypatrol/index.html).

University of Chicago News Office. "Most Americans Think People Need to
Be 26 to Be Considered Grown-Up: Seven Steps Toward Adulthood
Take Five Years. Norc Survey at University of Chicago Finds." May 9,
2003. (http://www.News.Uchicago.Edu/Releases/03/030509
.Adulthood.Shtml).

Commandment 9: Be Worldly

Lancy, David. *The Anthropology of Childhood: Cherubs, Chattel, Changelings.* New York: Cambridge University Press, 2008.

Commandment 10: Get Braver

Balter, Lawrence. (ed.). *Parenthood in America: An Encyclopedia.* Santa Barbara, Calif.: ABC-CLIO, 2000.

Stearns, Peter. *Anxious Parents: A History of Modern Childrearing in America.* New York: NYU Press, 2004.

Commandment 11: Relax

Breznican, Anthony. "Angelina and Clint See Eye to Eye; Famous Mother Had to Push Feelings Aside for Director's Kidnap Drama 'Changeling.'" *USA Today,* Oct. 16, 2008, p. 9b.

Bruer, John. *The Myth of the First Three Years: A New Understanding of Early Brain Development and Lifelong Learning.* New York: Free Press, 2002.

Harris, Judith Rich. *The Nurture Assumption: Why Children Turn Out the Way They Do.* New York: Touchstone, 1999.

Hirsh-Pasek, Kathy, and Roberta Michnick Golinkoff, with Diane Eyar. *Einstein Never Used Flash Cards: How Our Children Really Learn—and Why They Need to Play More and Memorize Less.* New York: Rodale Books, 2004.

Marano, Hara Estroff. *A Nation of Wimps: The High Cost of Invasive Parenting.* New York: Broadway Books, 2008.

UrbanBaby.com.

Commandment 12: Fail!

Bluefishtv. "Big Failures." (http://www.wimp.com/bigfailures/).

Dweck, Carol. *Mindset: The New Psychology of Success.* New York: Ballantine Books, 2007.

Grolnick, Wendy, and Kathy Seal. *Pressured Parents, Stressed-Out Kids: Dealing with Competition While Raising a Successful Child.* Amherst, N.Y.: Prometheus Books, 2008.

Rosenfeld, Alvin, and Nichole Wise. *The Over-Scheduled Child: Avoiding the Hyper-Parenting Trap.* New York: St. Martin's Griffin, 2001.

Commandment 13: Lock Them Out

Clements, Rhonda. "An Investigation of the Status of Outdoor Play." *Contemporary Issues in Early Childhood*, 2004, pp. 68–80.

Crimes Against Children Research Center (http://www.unh.edu/ccrc/).

Ginsburg, Kenneth R., the Committee on Communications, and the Committee on Psychosocial Aspects of Child and Family Health at the American Academy of Pediatrics. "The Importance of Play in Promoting Healthy Child Development and Maintaining Strong Parent-Child Bonds." Jan. 2007. (http://www.aap.org/pressroom/playFINAL.pdf).

Greenhearts Institute for Nature in Childhood. "An Annotated Bibliography for Nature Play." (http://www.greenheartsinc.org/uploads/Green _Hearts_annotated_bibliography_2.pdf).

Louv, Richard. *Last Child in the Woods: Saving Our Children from Nature-Deficit Disorder*. Chapel Hill, N.C.: Algonquin Books, 2005.

Sawyer, Keith. *Group Genius: The Creative Power of Collaboration*. New York: Basic Books, 2008.

Solomon, Pablo (www.pablosolomon.com).

Safe or Not? The A-to-Z Guide to Everything You Might Be Worried About

Animals (Being Eaten By)

Rubenstein, Steve. "Escaped Tiger Kills Visitor to S.F. Zoo." *San Francisco Chronicle*, Dec. 26, 2007, p. A1.

SFzoo.org.

Bats (Metal)

"Epidemiological Features of High School Baseball Injuries in the United States, 2005–2007." *Pediatrics*, June 2008, pp. 1181–1187.

"First Onfield Study Comparing Wood to Nonwood Bats Finds Both Safe. 'No Statistically Significant Difference in Injuries,' Says Illinois High School Study by School of Kinesiology and Recreation at Illinois State University." (http://www.dtmba.com/docs/New%20Field %20Study%20Shows%20NonWood%20Bats%20Safe.pdf).

"An Issue of Life and Death." *New York Times*, July 16, 2006, sports section, p. 1. (http://www.nytimes.com/2006/07/16/sports/baseball/16bats.html).

"Little League International Statement on Non-Wood Bats." (http://www .littleleague.org/media/newsarchive/Unknown_Dates/bats.htm).

"Wood and Metal Bats—USA Baseball Medical/Safety Advisory Committee" (youth baseball fatalities study), Mar. 27, 2007. (http://mlb.mlb.com/ usa_baseball/article.jsp?story=medsafety10).

Bottle Feeding: Formula for Disaster?

Goldein, Rebecca, Emer Smyth, and Andrea Foulkes. "What Science Really Says About the Benefits of Breast-Feeding." STATS.org, June 20, 2006. (http://stats.org/stories/breast_feed_nyt_jun_20_06.htm).

Gordon, Catherine M., and others. "Prevalence of Vitamin D Deficiency Among Healthy Infants and Toddlers." *Archives of Pediatrics and Adolescent Medicine,* June 2008, pp. 505–512.

Kramer, Michael S., and others from the Promotion of Breastfeeding Intervention Trial Study Group. "Effects of Prolonged and Exclusive Breastfeeding on Child Behavior and Maternal Adjustment: Evidence from a Large, Randomized Trial." *Pediatrics,* Mar. 2008, pp. e435–e440.

Kukla, Rebecca. "Ethics and Ideology in Breastfeeding Advocacy Campaigns." *Hypatia,* Winter 2006, *21*(1), 157–181.

BPA Poisoning Baby Bottles, Sippy Cups . . . and Everything Else

"Harvard Center for Risk Analysis Expert Panel Finds No Consistent Affirmative Evidence of Low-Dose BPA Effects." Sept. 3, 2004. (http://www .bisphenol-a.org/whatsNew/20040903Harvard.html).

McDermott, Nancy. "The Great American Baby Bottle Scare." Spiked-online .com. (http://www.spiked-online.com/index.php?/site/article/5179/).

Willhite, Calvin. "Bisphenol A and Public Health." June 10, 2008. Testimony prepared for U.S. House of Representatives. (http://energycommerce .house.gov/cmte_mtgs/110-ctcp-hrg.061008.Willhite-testimony.pdf).

Cell Phones and Brain Cancer

Watson, Richard. *Future Files: The 5 Trends that Will Shape the Next 50 Years.* London: Nicholas Brealey Publishing, 2008.

Choking on Food and All the Other Little Things Around the House

Centers for Disease Control and Prevention. "Nonfatal Choking-Related Episodes Among Children—United States, 2001." (http://www.cdc .gov/mmwr/preview/mmwrhtml/mm5142a1.htm).

"Holiday Safety Tips from the American Red Cross." (http://www.redcross
-semn.org/index.php?/Chapter-News/holiday-safety-tips-from-the
-american-red-cross.html).

Cough and Cold Medicinitis

Harris, Gardiner. "Experts Seek Ban on Cold Medicine for Very Young." *New York Times*, Sept. 29, 2007, p. 1A.

"Infant Deaths Associated with Cough and Cold Medications—Two States, 2005." *Journal of the American Medical Association*, Feb. 28, 2007, pp. 800–801.

OTCSafety.org. "Parents—Safe and Appropriate Dosing in Children." (http://www.otcsafety.org/content/?id=157).

Death by Stroller

Pavey, Ainsley. "Up to 200 Children Are Injured in Pram Accidents Each Year in Queensland, Statistics Show." *Sunday Mail* (Australia), Dec. 17, 2006, p. 5. (http://www.news.com.au/couriermail/story/0,23739 ,20939848-3102,00.html).

U.S. Consumer Product Safety Commission. "Infants Can Die When Their Heads Become Trapped in Strollers." Consumer Product Safety Alert. (http://www.cpsc.gov/cpscpub/pubs/5096.pdf).

U.S. Consumer Product Safety Commission. "Nursery Product-Related Injuries and Deaths to Children Under Age Five." (http://www.cpsc.gov/ LIBRARY/nursery05.pdf).

U.S. Consumer Product Safety Commission, Recalls and Product Safety News (http://www.cpsc.gov/cpscpub/prerel/prerel.html).

Eating Snow

Christner, Brent C., and others. "Ubiquity of Biological Ice Nucleators in Snowfall." *Science*, Feb. 29, 2008, p. 1214.

Germs, Anti-Germs, and Shopping Cart Liners

Adler, Alan J. "Study Shows Lower Asthma Rates Among Farm Children." (http://healthlink.mcw.edu/article/1031002434.html).

Braun-Fahrlander, C., and others. "Prevalence of Hay Fever and Allergic Sensitization in Farmer's Children and Their Peers Living in the Same Rural Community." *Clinical and Experimental Allergy*, 1999, *29*, 28–34. (http://www.ncbi.nlm.nih.gov/pubmed/10051699).

"Day Care Prevents Asthma." (http://www.connectwithkids.com/tipsheet/ 2008/405_oct1/thisweek/081001_asthma.shtml).

Strachan, David. "Hay Fever, Hygiene, and Household Size." *British Medical Journal*, Nov. 18, 1989, pp. 1259–1260. (http://www.pubmedcentral .nih.gov/articlerender.fcgi?artid=1838109).

Internet Predators and Other Skeeves Online

The Internet Safety Technical Task Force. "Enhancing Child Safety & Online Technologies." The Berkman Center for Internet & Society at Harvard University. Dec. 31, 2008. (http://cyber.law.harvard.edu/ sites/cyber.law.harvard.edu/files/ISTTF_Final_Report-Executive _Summary.pdf).

"Kids and Teen Online Safety." Love Our Children USA. (http://www.loveour childrenusa.org/kidsteens_onlinesafety.php).

National Center for Missing and Exploited Children. "Keeping Kids Safer on the Internet." (http://www.missingkids.com/missingkids/servlet/ ResourceServlet?LanguageCountry=en_US&PageId=2954).

Wolak, Janis, David Finkelhor, and Kimberly Mitchell. "1 in 7 Youth: The Statistics About Online Sexual Solicitations." Prepared for Crimes Against Children Research Center, Dec. 2007. (http://www.unh.edu/ ccrc/internet-crimes/factsheet_1in7.html).

Ybarra, Michele L., and Kimberly J. Mitchell. "How Risky Are Social Networking Sites? A Comparison of Places Online Where Youth Sexual Solicitation and Harassment Occurs." *Pediatrics*, Jan. 2008, pp. e350–e357.

Lead Paint, Lead Toys, and Lead Everything from China

Centers for Disease Control and Prevention. "Blood Lead Levels: United States, 1999–2002." Morbidity and Mortality Weekly Report. (http://www.cdc.gov/mmwr/preview/mmwrhtml/mm5420a5.html).

"Dangers of Lead Still Linger." *F.D.A. Consumer: The Magazine of the U.S. Food and Drug Administration*, Jan.-Feb. 1998. (http://www.fda.gov/ FDAC/features/1998/198_lead.html).

Mayo Clinic Staff. "Children's Health: Lead Poisoning." (http://www.mayo clinic.com/health/lead-poisoning/FL00068).

U.S. Environmental Protection Agency. "Pediatric Lead Poisoning: Is There a Threshold?" *Public Health Reports*. Nov.-Dec. 2000. (http://es.epa.gov/ ncer/childrenscenters/full_text/33615.pdf).

Vedantam, Shankar. "Research Links Lead Exposure, Criminal Activity." *Washington Post*, July 8, 2007, p. A2.

Plastic Bags and Why There Are Warnings All over Them

U.S. Consumer Product Safety Commission. "Children Still Suffocating with Plastic Bags." Consumer Product Safety Alert. (http://www.cpsc.gov/CPSCPUB/PUBS/5064.pdf).

Playground Perils

"It's Good for Children to Hurt Themselves at Play, Says Safety Charity Chief." *London Times*, Nov. 12, 2007, p. 13.

Tinsworth, Deborah K., and Joyce E. McDonald. "Special Study: Injuries and Deaths Associated with Children's Playground Equipment." U.S. Consumer Product Safety Commission. Apr. 2001. (http://www.cpsc.gov/LIBRARY/Playgrnd.pdf).

Pools and Water and Kids and Toilets (Not the Fun Part)

Safe Kids Pierce County. "Drowning and Water Related Safety." (http://safekidspiercecounty.health.officelive.com/Documents/Drowning%20Fact%20Sheet.pdf).

Safe Kids USA. "Injury Facts: Drowning." (http://usa.safekids.org/tier3_cd.cfm?folder_id=540&content_item_id=1032).

Safe Kids Worldwide. "Safety Tips: Water and Drowning Safety." (http://www.safekids.org/tips/tips_water.html).

U.S. Consumer Product Safety Commission. "CPSC Warns: Pools Are Not the Only Drowning Danger at Home for Kids—Data Show Other Hazards Cause More Than 100 Residential Child Drowning Deaths Annually." May 23, 2002. (http://www.cpsc.gov/cpscpub/prerel/prhtml02/02169.html).

Raw Dough's Raw Deal

Centers for Disease Control. "Outbreaks of *Salmonella* Serotype Enteritidis Infection Associated with Eating Raw or Undercooked Shell Eggs—United States, 1996–1998," Feb. 4, 2000. (http://www.cdc.gov/mmwr/preview/mmwrhtml/mm4904a1.htm#tab1).

Hope, B. K., and others. "An Overview of the Salmonella Enteritidis Risk Assessment for Shell Eggs and Egg Products." U.S. Dept of Agriculture, Food Safety and Inspection Service. (http://www.ncbi.nlm.nih.gov/pubmed/12022671).

School Shootings

"Controversy Erupts over School Proposal to Teach Kids to Fight Back Against Gunmen." *Fox News*, Dec. 10, 2008. (http://www.foxnews.com/story/0,2933,464848,00.html).

National Center for Education Statistics. "Indicators of School Crime and Safety: 2007." (http://nces.ed.gov/programs/crimeindicators/crime indicators2007/tables/table_01_1.asp).

National Center for Education Statistics. "Number of Student-Reported Nonfatal Crimes Against Students Ages 12–18 and Rate of Crimes per 1,000 Students, by Location and Year: 1992–2005." (http://nces.ed.gov/programs/crimeindicators/crimeindicators2007/tables/table_02_1.asp).

Spoilage (of Lunch)

O'Connor, Anahad. "The Claim: Mayonnaise Can Increase Risk of Food Poisoning." *New York Times*, July 1, 2008, science section, p. 5. (http://www.nytimes.com/2008/07/01/health/01real.html?pagewanted=print).

Rourke, Mickey. "Study Finds That Mayonnaise Can Inhibit Spoilage of Food." *New York Times*, May 12, 1982, Section C, p. 4. (http://Query.Nytimes.Com/Gst/Fullpage.Html?Sec=Health&Res=9d03e3d61438f931a257 56c0a964948260).

Sudden Infant Death Syndrome (SIDS)

Brosco, J. P. "The Early History of the Infant Mortality Rate in America: A Reflection Upon the Past and a Prophecy of the Future." *Pediatrics*, Feb. 1999, pp. 478–485.

Centers for Disease Control and Prevention. "Achievements in Public Health, 1900–1999: Healthier Mothers and Babies." *Morbidity and Mortality Weekly Report*, Oct. 1, 1999. (http://www.cdc.gov/mmwr/preview/mmwrhtml/mm4838a2.html).

"Positioning and Sudden Infant Death Syndrome (SIDS) Update." *Pediatrics*, Dec. 6,1996, pp. 1216–1218. (http://pediatrics.aappublications.org/cgi/content/abstract/98/6/1216?maxtoshow=&HITS=10&hits=10&R ESULTFORMAT=&titleabstract=task%252Bforce%252Bon%252 Binfant%252Bsleep%252Bpositioning&searchid=1049232258104 _6231&stored_search=&FIRSTINDEX=0&fdate=1/1/1992&tdate =12/31/2002&journalcode=pediatrics).

Task American Academy of Pediatrics. Force on Sudden Infant Death Syndrome. "The Changing Concept of Sudden Infant Death Syndrome." *Pediatrics*, Nov. 2005, pp. 1245–1255. (http://aappolicy.aappublications.org/cgi/content/full/pediatrics;116/5/1245).

U.S. Consumer Product Safety Commission. "Retailers Join CPSC in Promoting Safe Bedding Practices for Babies—Each Year 900 SIDS Deaths May Be Caused by Soft Bedding." News from CPSC, Mar. 14, 2000. (http://www.cpsc.gov/CPSCPUB/PREREL/prhtml00/00078.html).

"U.S. Policy: 'Back to Sleep' for Babies." *New York Times*, June 22, 1994. (http://query.nytimes.com/gst/fullpage.html?sec=health&res=9500EFD9103DF931A15755C0A962958260).

Sunscreen, Vitamin D, Skin Cancer, You Name It

American Academy of Pediatrics. "Summer Safety Tips—Part I." (http://www.aap.org/advocacy/releases/summertips.cfm).

American Cancer Society. "Cancer Facts and Figures 2008." (http://www.cancer.org/downloads/STT/2008CAFFfinalsecured.pdf).

American Cancer Society. "Skin Cancer Prevention and Early Detection." (http://www.cancer.org/docroot/PED/content/ped_7_1_Skin_Cancer_Detection_What_You_Can_Do.asp?sitearea=&level=).

Gartner, Lawrence M., and Frank R. Greer. Section on Breastfeeding and Committee on Nutrition. "Prevention of Rickets and Vitamin D Deficiency: New Guidelines for Vitamin D Intake." *Pediatrics*, Aug. 2008. (http://aappolicy.aappublications.org/cgi/content/full/pediatrics;111/4/908).

Mayo Clinic Staff. "Rickets." (http://www.mayoclinic.com/print/rickets/DS00813/).

Misra, Madhusmita, and others, on behalf of the Drug and Therapeutics Committee of the Lawson Wilkins Pediatric Endocrine Society. "Vitamin D Deficiency in Children and Its Management: Review of Current Knowledge and Recommendations." *Pediatrics*, Aug. 2008, pp. 398–417. (http://pediatrics.aappublications.org/cgi/content/abstract/122/2/398?maxtoshow=&HITS=10&hits=10&RESULTFORMAT=&fulltext=vitamin+d&andorexactfulltext=and&searchid=1&FIRSTINDEX=0&sortspec=relevance&resourcetype=HWCIT).

Teen Sex (Yes, Kids, We Know You're Reading This. Now Come and Ask Us All About Contraception)

National Campaign to Prevent Teen and Unplanned Pregnancy. "Teen Sexual Activity in the United States." (http://www.thenationalcampaign.org/national-data/pdf/TeenSexActivityOnePagerJune06.pdf).

The Woods, Playing In

"The Great Outdoors." *Parents*, May 2008.
Louv, Richard. *Last Child in the Woods: Saving Our Children from Nature-Deficit Disorder*. Chapel Hill, N.C.: Algonquin Books, 2005.

Walking to School (or at Least the Bus Stop)

Centers for Disease Control and Prevention. KidsWalk-to-School. "Then and Now—Barriers and Solutions." (http://www.cdc.gov/nccdphp/Dnpa/kidswalk/then_and_now.htm).
National Center for Safe Routes to School (Saferoutesinfo.org).
PedNet Coalition (www.pednet.org/).

Strangers with Candy

ASSERT Super Kids (http://assertnow.net/).
"Clear Danger: A National Study of Childhood Drowning and Related Attitudes and Behaviors." Safe Kids USA. Apr. 2004. (http://www.usa.safekids.org/NSKW.cfm).
Crimes Against Children Research Center (http://www.unh.edu/ccrc/).
Crimes Against Children Research Center crime trends statistics (http://www.unh.edu/ccrc/Trends/index.html).
Crimes Against Children Research Center kidnapping statistics (http://www.unh.edu/ccrc/kidnapping/).
Emberly, Edward R. *Go Away, Big Green Monster!* New York: Little, Brown, 1993.
Finkelhor, David. "The Great Interpersonal Violence Decline." Presentation at the American Psychological Association Interpersonal Violence Summit, Bethesda, Md., Feb. 2008.
Finkelhor, David, Heather Hammer, and Andrea J. Sedlak. "Nonfamily Abducted Children: National Estimates and Characteristics." Prepared for the U.S. Department of Justice. (http://www.ncjrs.gov/pdffiles1/ojjdp/196467.pdf).
National Center for Missing and Exploited Children (www.missingkids.com).
National Highway Traffic Administration Safety statistics, crunched by Fatality Analysis Reporting System (http://www-fars.nhtsa.dot.gov/People/PeopleAllVictims.aspx).
U.S. Consumer Product Safety Commission. "CPSC Warns: Pools Are Not the Only Drowning Danger at Home for Kids—Data Show Other Hazards Cause More Than 100 Residential Child Drowning Deaths Annually." May 23, 2002. (http://www.cpsc.gov/cpscpub/prerel/prhtml02/02169.html).

U.S. Department of Justice, Office of Justice Programs, Bureau of Justice
    Statistics. "Young Adults Have the Highest Homicide Victimization
    and Offending Rates." (www.ojp.usdoj.gov/bjs/homicide/teens.htm).
U.S. Fire Administration."Fire Risks to Children in 2004." Feb. 2008. (http://
    www.usfa.dhs.gov/downloads/pdf/tfrs/v7i6.pdf).

Conclusion

Derbyshire, David. "How Children Lost the Right to Roam in Four Genera-
    tions." *Daily Mail*, June 15, 2007. (http://www.dailymail.co.uk/news/
    article-462091/How-children-lost-right-roam-generations.html).
Friedan, Betty. *The Feminine Mystique*. New York: Norton, 2001.
Twadell, Eric. "The Self-Esteem Movement Is Fading." *Minuteman*, Sept. 2008,
    pp. 4–5.

Helpful Books, Blogs, Web Sites, and Some Inspiring Family Movies

Books

Cairns, Warwick. *How to Live Dangerously: Why We Should All Stop Worrying and Start Living*. London: Macmillan, 2008.

Furedi, Frank. *Paranoid Parenting: Why Ignoring the Experts May Be Best for Your Child*. Chicago: Chicago Review Press, 2002.

Gardner, Daniel. *The Science of Fear: Why We Fear the Things We Shouldn't—and Put Ourselves in Greater Danger*. New York: Dutton, 2008.

Grolnick, Wendy, and Kathy Seal. *Pressured Parents, Stressed-Out Kids: Dealing with Competition While Raising a Successful Child*. Amherst, N.Y.: Prometheus Books, 2008.

Harris, Judith Rich. *The Nurture Assumption: Why Children Turn Out the Way They Do*. New York: Touchstone, 1999.

Hicks, Marybeth. *Bringing Up Geeks—Genuine, Enthusiastic, Empowered Kids: How to Protect Your Kid's Childhood in a Grow-Up-Too-Fast World*. New York: Berkeley Books, 2008.

Honoré, Carl. *Under Pressure: Rescuing Our Children from the Culture of Hyper-Parenting*. New York: HarperOne, 2008.

Howard, Philip K. *Life Without Lawyers: Liberating Americans from Too Much Law*. New York: Norton, 2009.

Jackson, Maggie. *Distracted: The Erosion of Attention and the Coming Dark Age*. Amherst, N.Y.: Prometheus Books, 2008.

Levitt, Steven D., and Stephen J. Dubner, *Freakonomics: A Rogue Economist Explores the Hidden Side of Everything*. (Rev. ed.) New York:: Morrow, 2006.

Linn, Susan. *The Case for Make Believe: Saving Play in a Commercialized World.*
    New York: New Press, 2008.
Linn, Susan. *Consuming Kids: Protecting Our Children from the Onslaught of Marketing and Advertising.* New York: Anchor, 2005.
Louv, Richard. *Last Child in the Woods: Saving Our Children from Nature-Deficit Disorder.* Chapel Hill, N.C.: Algonquin Books, 2005.
Marano, Hara Estroff. *A Nation of Wimps: The High Cost of Invasive Parenting.*
    New York: Broadway Books, 2008.
Mintz, Steven. *Huck's Raft: A History of American Childhood.* Cambridge,
    Mass.: Belknap Press, 2006.
Paul, Pamela. *Parenting, Inc.: How We Are Sold on $800 Strollers, Fetal Education, Baby Sign Language, Sleeping Coaches, Toddler Couture, and Diaper Wipe Warmers—and What It Means for Our Children.* New York: Times Books, 2008.
Ross, John F. *The Polar Bear Strategy: Reflections on Risk in Modern Life.* Reading,
    Mass.: Perseus Books, 1999.
Singer, Jen. *Stop Second-Guessing Yourself—the Toddler Years: A Field-Tested Guide to Confident Parenting.* Deerfield Beach, Fla.: HCI Books, 2009.
Spock, Benjamin, and Robert Needlman. *Dr. Spock's Baby and Child Care.* (8th ed.) New York: Pocket Books, 2004.
Stearns, Peter. *Anxious Parents: A History of Modern Childrearing in America.*
    New York: NYU Press, 2004.

Blogs

The Compass (http://www.marybethhicks.com/blog.aspx)
Mommy Myth Buster (http://mommymythbuster.wordpress.com/)
Motherlode: Adventures in Parenting (http://parenting.blogs.nytimes.com/)
Ordinary Kid (www.ordinarykid.com)
School Gate (British) (http://timesonline.typepad.com/schoolgate/)

Web Sites

Café Mom (http://www.cafemom.com/)
Carl Honoré, author of *Under Pressure* (http://www.carlhonore.com/)
Cool Mom (http://coolmom.com/)
Crimes Against Children Research Center (http://www.unh.edu/ccrc/)
The Family Groove (http://thefamilygroove.com/)
Honest Baby (http://www.honestbaby.com/)
Momma Said (Jen Singer) (http://mommasaid.net/)
Spiked Online (search for Nancy McDermott) (http://www.spiked-online
    .com/SPIKED)
STATS.org (http://stats.org/)

Some Inspiring Family Movies

Akeelah and the Bee

Anne of Green Gables

Annie

Because of Winn-Dixie

The Black Stallion

The Chronicles of Narnia series

Harry Potter series

Holes

My Side of the Mountain

October Sky

Oliver! (the 1968 musical)

Secret Life of Bees

Shiloh

To Kill a Mockingbird

Whale Rider

About the Author

Lenore Skenazy grew up pretty much Free Range in the suburbs of Chicago, and even though it wasn't that eventful, she has been trying to give her two sons that same kind of childhood ever since.

When not busy encouraging their independence (even while shouting, "Don't listen to your iPod while crossing the street!"), she writes an unpredictable op-ed column that appears in more than one hundred papers and takes a skeptical look at the culture that has brought us bottled water for dogs, pole dancing for grannies, and an SAT vocabulary shower curtain for kids.

Her observations can be heard on NPR and read regularly in *Advertising Age* and *Reader's Digest*. She has also written for *Mad* magazine and coauthored *The Dysfunctional Family Christmas Songbook* and the quiz book *Who's the Blonde That Married What's-His-Name?* Her humor contest, "What Next?" runs in *The Week* magazine. She also spent several years on TV as a (younger, cuter) Andy Rooney, at CNBC and the Food Network.

After she wrote about letting her nine-year-old ride the subway alone, she found herself on *The Today Show*, *Dr. Phil*, and the BBC, defending herself against charges that she's "America's Worst Mom." She launched the blog Free-Range Kids to explain her parenting philosophy and went on to write the book you're holding. Or maybe it's sitting on the table in front of you and you're reading it while drinking a cup of coffee. That would be even nicer.

Skenazy lives in Manhattan with her husband, Joe Kolman, and those more-or-less Free-Range sons of theirs, Morry and Izzy. Contact her at freerangekids.com.

Index

FREE-RANGE KIDS
MEMBERSHIP CARDS

Clip 'n Save!
Or Make Copies for You and Your Friends!

I'm not lost, I am a

Free-Range Kid!

I have been taught how to cross the street safely. I know never to GO OFF with strangers, but I can talk to them. I like being outside and exploring the world. If you are a grown-up, you probably did the same things when you were a kid, so please do not be alarmed. The adults in my life know where I am, but if you want to talk to them, feel free to give them a call.

The number is: _____.

Have a Free-Range Day!

(Signed) _____

www.freerangekids.com

I am a Free-Range Parent

I believe in teaching children to be safe and then giving them the freedom we had as kids. If you think times are more dangerous today, please take a look at these statistics:

- **36% decline in homicides of children under age 14, 1993–2005** (Source: U.S. Dept. of Justice)
- **60% decline in homicides of children ages 14–17, 1993–2005** (Source: U.S. Dept. of Justice)
- **79% decline in juvenile sex victimization trends, 1993–2003** (Source: National Crime Victimization Survey)
- **Each year, about 2,000 children are killed as passengers in cars. About 50 are kidnapped and killed by strangers.** That means children are 40 times more likely to die in a car trip to the mall than during a walk home from school.

Raising confident, competent kids is my goal. Thanks for understanding.

(Signed) _____

www.freerangekids.com